C000054554

797,885 Books

are available to read at

www.ForgottenBooks.com

Forgotten Books' App
Available for mobile, tablet & eReader

ISBN 978-1-331-14803-6
PIBN 10150636

This book is a reproduction of an important historical work. Forgotten Books uses
state-of-the-art technology to digitally reconstruct the work, preserving the original format
whilst repairing imperfections present in the aged copy. In rare cases, an imperfection in
the original, such as a blemish or missing page, may be replicated in our edition. We do,
however, repair the vast majority of imperfections successfully; any imperfections that
remain are intentionally left to preserve the state of such historical works.

Forgotten Books is a registered trademark of FB &c Ltd.
Copyright © 2017 FB &c Ltd.
FB &c Ltd, Dalton House, 60 Windsor Avenue, London, SW19 2RR.
Company number 08720141. Registered in England and Wales.

For support please visit www.forgottenbooks.com

1 MONTH OF
FREE
READING

at

www.ForgottenBooks.com

By purchasing this book you are eligible for one month membership to ForgottenBooks.com, giving you unlimited access to our entire collection of over 700,000 titles via our web site and mobile apps.

To claim your free month visit: www.forgottenbooks.com/free150636

* Offer is valid for 45 days from date of purchase. Terms and conditions apply.

English
Français
Deutsche
Italiano
Español
Português

www.forgottenbooks.com

Mythology Photography **Fiction**
Fishing Christianity **Art** Cooking
Essays Buddhism Freemasonry
Medicine **Biology** Music **Ancient
Egypt** Evolution Carpentry Physics
Dance Geology **Mathematics** Fitness
Shakespeare **Folklore** Yoga Marketing
Confidence Immortality Biographies
Poetry **Psychology** Witchcraft
Electronics Chemistry History **Law**
Accounting **Philosophy** Anthropology
Alchemy Drama Quantum Mechanics
Atheism Sexual Health **Ancient History**
Entrepreneurship Languages Sport
Paleontology Needlework Islam
Metaphysics Investment Archaeology
Parenting Statistics Criminology
Motivational

CERTAIN DANGEROUS TENDENCIES IN AMERICAN LIFE, AND OTHER PAPERS.

[by
[Jonathan Baxter Harrison]

BOSTON:
HOUGHTON, OSGOOD AND COMPANY.
The Riverside Press, Cambridge.
1880.

Copyright, 1880,
By HOUGHTON, OSGOOD & CO.

All rights reserved.

RIVERSIDE, CAMBRIDGE:
STEREOTYPED AND PRINTED BY
H. O. HOUGHTON AND COMPANY

CONTENTS.

My neighbor, who was the possessor of fifty thousand dollars, bought a piece of land for eight thousand, and built on it a house which cost him nearly all his remaining fortune. He seemed to think that the money he had changed into stone walls, fine carvings, and costly furniture would still be productive, would yield him an income. When he had thus improved the property, as he phrased it, he claimed that it was worth at least sixty thousand dollars; that is, he had spent most of his money and thought he was worth much more than when he began. He has some high-priced European paintings, but he cannot eat them, and as he has nothing but his house and grounds he has had to stint his children in their education, and even in their clothes and food. He wishes to sell his property, but thinks it still worth fifty thousand dollars, though it would not sell for one third of that amount. This is a pretty good representation of the course of multitudes of business men. The result is that the country is vastly poorer than the people are willing to admit; that is, they value their property at vastly more than it is really worth. Much of our wealth consists of houses, furniture, mills, machinery, and railroads which produce nothing, and which cannot be sold. This is not real wealth. Much of the money invested in such things is irretrievably lost, and it would be better for us to face the disagreeable truth at once.

This extravagance and the delusion which fos-

tered it had some important results in the domain
of morals. Manual labor came to be regarded as
in great measure unnecessary, and to be despised
as a badge of inferiority by many who had always
been engaged in it. Multitudes of men who had
until then honestly earned or produced their living by the work of their hands now began to live
by their wits, by starting and controlling business
enterprises for the investment of other people's
money, and by taking government contracts and
corporation jobs. The abounding dishonesty which
has since then been our curse, the repudiation of
the debts of States, towns, and cities, with the
alarming development of the disposition to steal
trust funds, — these and other unfavorable elements in the life of the time had their source and
main impulse in the delusion about the nature and
powers of paper money, in the uncertainty of its
value, and in the extravagance engendered by the
war. A passionate greed for riches was developed
among our people. Men had no longer any vision
for realities, but built upon illusions and impossibilities as if they were the solid facts and laws of
nature. The leading clergymen and writers of
the nation encouraged and defended this enormous and reckless acquisitiveness, and talked, in
philosophical phrases, about the aspirations of the
masses for improved conditions, leisure for culture, and a higher civilization. The pulpit gave
to luxury the sanction of religion, and the press
urged the people onward in their career of extrav-

with anybody's money. They will do what they
believe to be right, though all men deride or oppose, and at any cost to themselves in business or
worldly interests. But they are too few to regen-
erate the American church, though their influence
is highly valuable in resisting some of the evil
tendencies of the age. Most of them are old, and
they have few successors among the younger people. They have already done most of their work,
and their number and strength diminish from
year to year.

For a very large class of which we may next
speak the church furnishes opportunity for a
pleasant social life, which is in no way different
from the social life of amiable, intelligent people
out of the church; that is, there is nothing dis-
tinctively religious about it. For this class all the
barriers and distinctions between the church and
the world have been removed. Church work is
for them, in all its forms, a kind of sacred amusement. Public worship, with its pulpit oratory
and modern church music, is an æsthetic entertainment. They have developed a religion which
is not religious. They have learned how to be
Christians, according to their meaning, without
self-denial, or any abridgment of the pleasures,
pursuits, or ambitions of people who acknowledge
no religious obligations. They are the most intelligent members of the popular churches of this
country. They are decorously moral, conforming
to the easy, worldly criterion of people of like so-

cial position. They are nearly all able to live comfortably, possessing the necessaries of life and a few of its luxuries. They are not usually scrupulously truthful or conscientious, and do not believe it possible to maintain a very high standard of justice or honesty in business life. They regard the golden rule as impracticable, and with more or less sincerity deplore the existence of insurmountable obstacles in the way of obeying it. They do not believe the creeds which they subscribe when they join the church, and generally make no secret afterward of their doubt or disbelief respecting various fundamental doctrines of Christianity. But they have a horror of all dissent which takes a man out of the popular church, and show no respect for the plea of conscience in such cases. They are all optimists, believing that things are sure to come out right. They distrust personal earnestness in religious matters, but are capable of self-sacrifice or action for the public good in ways approved by their class, while they are without the qualities or temper enabling a man to serve an unpopular principle or cause. They give largely for all kinds of charities. In them the religion popularly professed has spent its force, and they can contribute little to aid in the moral regeneration of the country. They are almost destitute of moral insight, and have little confidence in principles, trusting entirely to management, to policy, and to present success.

Their ministers are men of intelligence and of

considerable culture. They believe even less than their people of the doctrines of their creeds. They generally avoid doctrinal subjects in preaching, and have for some years based their teaching mostly upon utilitarian grounds. They have for themselves accepted rationalistic beliefs far in advance of what they teach, and consider themselves engaged in a most necessary and useful work, — that of leading the people gradually onward in thought and knowledge by carefully giving them the truth as they are able to bear it. Their caution is extreme, and they thus sacrifice whatever strength may belong to courage and outspoken sincerity. Their teaching is far less advanced and rationalistic than the habitual thought of their hearers. They do not understand the real tendencies of the time, lacking the insight and the synthetic judgment which result from independent search for truth, and from heartiness of conviction. They greatly overrate the success of their system of repression, — of keeping back most of what they themselves believe. It fosters skepticism, and spreads distrust of all moral and religious verity, as the people are aware that their ministers practice the concealment of their real beliefs. Their preaching is usually far more intellectual than formerly, but is not based on the creeds, nor on any announced or coherent philosophy, fragments of hostile systems of thought often appearing in amiable proximity, if not in any real relation, to each other. There is nobody to criticise the preaching of these clergymen. Their teaching is often curiously remote from all the practical concerns and conditions of life in our time and country, and is almost entirely destitute of moral authority and power. They regard the general engagement of their people in the work of charity organizations as evidence of the triumphant vitality of Christianity in our age; which is much as if the officers of an army should boast that all their soldiers able for duty are in the hospitals caring for their sick comrades, and that all the able-bodied men at home must soon be conscripted for the same service. They do not see that Christianity, to be successful, must learn how to dry up, in great measure, the sources of the rising currents of pauperism, vice, and crime, nor understand that their own methods are largely responsible for the magnitude of the burdens, rapidly becoming intolerable, of the charities which are their pride.

In the more prosperous American churches in the regions to which modern styles of dress and living have extended there are now but few poor people, and these feel more and more each year that the church is no home for them. There is for them, usually, no fraternal association with their more fortunate neighbors in the church; no wholesome, natural, cordial relation between them as human beings or brethren. And there is a very large class who are not extremely poor, but who are obliged to dress plainly and to practice rigid economy in order to obtain the necessaries of life. In favorable times they may be said to rise to conditions of comfort, but for the most part they are familiar with the pressure of hardship, and their life is a struggle for the means to live. They of course cannot aspire to what is now considered good social position, as that usually depends upon the style·of dress and house-furnishing more than upon character. This is a very important portion of our population. Most of them are industrious and honest, and many of them are advancing in intelligence. Some of them have a strong desire for knowledge, and read the best books they can obtain. There is good material among them for a more rational and practical culture than is yet possessed by their neighbors who are in better circumstances. This class also is rapidly passing out of the church. The movement is largely the result of impulses from the more prosperous people in the churches, and is not caused so much by the growth of irreligion among these men and their families as by the development of an unfraternal spirit, — a class-feeling, — among those more successful in acquiring this world's goods. Many who are thus separating themselves from the churches are injured by the change. They enjoy their greater freedom from restraint, and often sink to a life of less strenuous effort at self-direction. They do not feel bound to resist temptation, or deny appetite its gratifications. But most of this class are still, in the main, moral and wholesome in character and personal influence, chiefly from the power of habit and family traditions of rectitude. Many of them are gradually becoming hostile and bitter toward the church and all specifically religious activities, and their children usually receive at home no religious instruction whatever, being free to go to church or not, as they please. The effect of this parental indifference upon the culture and morals of the young people is not favorable. Among the more intelligent of this class there has been, within the last fifteen years, a rapid development of what is called infidelity; that is, of opinions which involve the rejection of evangelical Christianity. Up to this time the great mass of plain people in this country, of those who work with their hands, know nothing of any religion besides evangelical Protestantism and Roman Catholicism. The people who reject the popular religious creeds, both among the poor and among the more prosperous and cultivated, with some exceptions to be noted farther on, are generally giving up religion entirely. No new system or form of religious belief or life is taking the place of the old faith which has lost its power. But these people are still accessible to any vital improving influences not specifically ecclesiastical in form. Their morals are commonly as good as those of the most prominent church-members, and they are probably more truthful, conscientious, and just than most people in the church. But they are not religious; that is, they have no ideas, principles, or beliefs in regard to human responsibility which exercise any considerable power of restraint upon their conduct when interest or appetite is involved. They feel no impulse to association with their neighbors for any kind of moral or religious culture. A few are inclined to propagate their negative notions and hostility to religion ; the greater number are simply indifferent. Many of them have read the newspaper and magazine dilutions of the writings of Darwin, Huxley, and Spencer, and have thus been strengthened in their opposition to the old beliefs. Most of them are sensible, practical, capable people, not given to sentiment or illusions of any kind ; often somewhat narrow and hard, but with valuable intellectual and moral qualities. Their greatest defect seems to be that they feel too little responsibility for the moral culture of their children and those of their neighbors. They have too little aspiration and national feeling, and are giving themselves entirely to material interests. It cannot be said that they are as a class doing much for themselves, and nobody else is doing anything for them as to culture or morals. Their future course depends upon that of the cultivated classes. If there is within a few years a marked expansion of national culture and increase of its dynamic vitality, these people will do much to strengthen the better tendencies of the nation's life. They are capable of important changes.

Below these as to intellectual character and

equipment there is a larger class, in whom prehistoric or savage thought still survives with very
slight modifications from science or any other
modern influence. Our fellow-citizens of this class
believe in luck, omens, dreams, signs of many
kinds (that is, in supernatural indications or fore-
shadowings of future events), and in the presence
and influence of the spirits of the dead, whom
they habitually or occasionally consult in various
ways. These have not all rejected evangelical
Protestantism, as great numbers of them are members of the popular churches. Many of them have
wealth and social position. The women of this
class constitute the larger portion of the great
army of readers of worthless books of fiction and
serials in the story-newspapers. Perhaps a majority of the members of the evangelical Protest-
ant churches in this country have at some time
consulted the spirits of dead people, by the help of
some professional ghost-seer or medium. But outside of the church the believers in spirits, spells,
possessions, omens, visions, warnings, and the
other features of prehistoric supernaturalism are
usually hostile to Christianity. They think the
inspirations and revelations of many trance-speakers and mediums in this country superior in value
to those recorded in the Bible. They have usually a scorn of history, and of the past as a
teacher, and are especially hostile to belief in any
authority except that of the individual soul. They
mostly regard society as a great oppressor, and be-

lieve that priests (they call all ministers priests) have been the authors and are now the chief supporters of nearly all the evils which afflict mankind. They are all sentimentalists ; that is, they attach little value to facts, and do not think it important to study them. Their contempt for scientific methods of investigation is nearly equal to their scorn for history. They depend chiefly upon intuition and the great instincts of humanity for their guidance, and for the determination of all problems. They would like to see the existing organization and institutions of society displaced, and think it would be a great gain to stop trying to patch up the old systems of religion and law, and begin anew. They see no great difficulty in the attempt to establish an entirely new organization of society, with all necessary institutions, machinery, and activities, and believe that it could be done at once, with immense advantage to the people, if only the priests and the money power were put down. They have a kind of rage against churches and all the organized activities of Christianity. They have not yet any religion of their own, in the modern sense of the word, as they do not worship or revere anything as higher or better than themselves. Their nearest approach to adoration is their belief in the omnipotence of a free platform ; that is, of a mass-meeting of believers in the sovereignty of the individual, with absolutely no restrictions as to the direction or extent of the discussions. They have a stronger impulse to propagate their sentiments than is manifested by any other class in our country at present, and have more enthusiasm and self-sacrifice for their cause and objects than the people who hold better doctrines. (This stirring of powerful impulses among the more ignorant and undeveloped, while the cultivated classes, the leaders of society, are bewildered and indisposed to action, is one of the most significant features of our age.) They have not wholly escaped injury to their morals in thus casting off the restraints of the old beliefs. There has been a serious and general lowering of moral tone and quality among them during the last fifteen years, and this deterioration is still going on. But this has not yet resulted in any great increase of concrete immorality, except the immorality of worthless talk, incessant, universal, and interminable. There has been some sexual vice among them, but it has been mostly of a cold-blooded kind, the effort of theorists making experiments and ostentatiously trying to be wicked, rather than the wild play of ungoverned impulse and passion. There is not yet a large growth of licentiousness in American society. It increases only as the criminal classes increase, and especially as thieves become more numerous. Thieves of all grades, burglars, and pickpockets habitually resort to houses of ill-fame. It is the common method of spending money dishonestly obtained. But there is not yet any considerable spread of licentiousness upward through society, and life is probably cleaner and better in this respect in our time than ever before. In other ways the immoral effects produced by the ideas and sentiments of the large class which I am now describing are extensive and important. They have seriously weakened respect for law in all parts of our country, and have profoundly influenced public sentiment in opposition to the punishment of criminals. They have to a great extent abjured the doctrine of individual responsibility for wrong-doing, and their ideas have pervaded the atmosphere of the age, and have so benumbed the conscience of the nation that the unwillingness of good people to have the laws enforced, and their sympathy for criminals, are among the most threatening evils of our society. Their worst immorality is their teaching; especially the character of their addresses, lectures, and discussions, in which there is almost everywhere a wild vehemence of attack upon all the principles of religion, morality, and social order, which is unrestrained by any regard for truth, decency, or justice. The orators are absolutely irresponsible, as they recognize no authority but their own wills. They have a fluency of extempore utterance, with ability to talk for any length of time, which inspires great admiration among the people ; for the masses in our country have a boundless delight in what they call eloquence, meaning usually a great flow of words and a confident manner, with many sounding phrases about the progress of humanity, the grandeur of free thought, and the resistless uprising of the people. No other class is at present so successfully educating the people of this country. They are positive and aggressive, and have a certain power of enthusiasm or afflatus which no other class now possesses. They have many organized societies, traveling lecturers, and missionaries, and a score or two of newspapers, besides an enormous literature of their own, if one may apply the word literature to their productions. It is a great and successful movement for the propagation of uneducated thought, the spectacle of the untaught classes and disorganizing forces of the time taking possession of the printing-press, of the rostrum, and of the ballot, and attacking modern society with its own weapons. It is a wide-spread revolt against civilization.

There can be no doubt, after any real investigation of the matter, that this class in whom the methods and tendencies of prehistoric thought are still dominant and almost unmodified by modern culture — the class believing in omens, visions, spirit communications, impressions, and intuitions, and in the sovereignty of the individual's impulses — includes several millions of our countrymen. They incline to think nearly all labor unnecessary, and generally regard employers as oppressors who defraud the workingmen of the larger part of the fruits of their toil. They are met and reinforced upon this ground by a great number of the working-class, who have no theories or ideas of progress, but who have done little honest work since the great inflation of prices a few years ago. That inflation had a most disastrous effect on the conscience and sense of honor of multitudes of workingmen. They have ever since acted on the plan of getting all they possibly can out of their employers, and giving as little as possible in return. They regard the capitalist, that is, whoever has money, as their natural enemy and prey. The theorists who wish to reconstruct society outright, and govern it afterward by mass-meetings in continuous session, encourage the discontent and indolence of the men who believe they ought to be paid high wages for very light work. The prostration of business and industry extending over the whole country during the last few years has given all these people unprecedented opportunity, and has greatly stimulated the sentiments and tendencies which they represent. They have the immense advantage and sanction which their attack upon the existing order of things derives from the extreme hardship and real suffering now for some time endured by many of the working people in different parts of our country.

The political objects and plans of this large class of our citizens are much more fully defined and articulate than is yet believed by those who regard them with contempt or indifference. Of course they do not themselves know what their own part may be in later stages of the enterprise which they are undertaking. But some of their aims are clear. They believe that the interests of the laborer, of the people, as they say, will be advanced by crippling and injuring capital in every possible way; and this they intend to do. They will influence legislation in this direction wherever they have the power. They do not regard the capitalist as one of the people, but as a criminal and enemy who has no rights that the people should respect. Those who possess property and who live in comfort and refinement are more and more regarded as the foes of the workingmen. Intellectual labor is not respected. Professional men, scholars, teachers, and cultivated people are none of them acknowledged as laborers, or as having any just title to labor's rewards. The relations between the people who have property and culture, on the one hand, and the workingmen, on the other, are regarded by the latter more and more as a state of war; so that any advantage gained or injury inflicted by the laborers is to be regarded as justifiable and right. We are in the earlier stages of a war upon property, and upon everything that satisfies what are called the higher wants of civilized life. The workingmen are taught to regard works of art and instruments of high culture, with all the possessions and surroundings of people of wealth and refinement, as causes and symbols of the laborer's poverty and degradation, and therefore as things to be hated. The movement has already in many places attacked and crippled the higher departments of our public-school education, and its leaders assail all endowments and appropriations for scientific research. The strongest tendencies and influences now operating among these people are leading them to a region and condition in which regard for the higher elements of the life of civilized man, for art, literature, and culture, is impossible. They do not value science more than art or religion, except in those applications of it which have an immediate commercial value. The war against all these things will be prosecuted with desperate energy and persistence unless something is speedily done to counteract and change some of the chief tendencies of the age ; unless there is an evolution or application of forces adequate to create a new series of circumstances. The instincts of destruction are already very strong in multitudes of men in this country. They are becoming fiercely hostile to everything that does not belong to the material life of man, or which is not required to satisfy his bodily wants.

The greatest danger is not that of armed violence or riotous destruction of property. The chief point of attack, naturally, and as arranged by the leaders of the movement, is to be for some time to come the money or currency of the country. They have for some years endeavored to bring the whole subject of the currency, its character, basis, and amount, under the direct and immediate control of the people in mass-meeting assembled, so that all questions of the issue and circulation of money shall be brought before the country, voted upon, and decided anew at every election. At present the leaders favor a series of feints, that is, strenuous advocacy of some measure that cannot be adopted ; and, when it is defeated, the attempt, without attracting attention or exciting opposition, to obtain in another form as nearly as possible the same legislation. Unless there is more effective effort to prevent such a result, our experience of a vast inflation of the currency, with the slow and painful climbing up again to specie payments, is likely to be repeated. There never was much purpose or coöperation among people of this class in our country until very recently, but they are now awaking to a sense of their power. Their idea of government is to place less emphasis upon constitutional provisions, to disregard or set them aside when necessary, and to depend more and more upon congressional legislation ; to make the judiciary and all other offices elective, to increase as much as may be the power of Congress, or rather of the House of Representatives, and to place, as nearly as possible, the entire administration of the government directly in the hands of the people, to be conducted by means of the political canvass or campaign. The aim is to destroy, little by little, the constitutional and representative character of the government, in order to enable the people to decide everything anew, if they wish to do so, at each annual election. There is to be an agitation or series of efforts for the reduction of all terms of office to the shortest possible time. Our fellow-citizens of this class hold that representatives of the people should always obey instructions from their constituents, or should immediately resign. They do not trust each other very far, and the workingmen especially believe that if one of their own number is elected to a place in a state legislature, or in Congress, he can be bribed or " bought up " by the money power, and that for a very paltry sum. They never before had any competent directors ; but while they still quarrel among themselves over details, a vast number are for the first time in substantial agreement in their purpose to seek the ends which I have described, and to advance toward them persistently, and by any methods that promise partial success. They hold that it is the function of government to " make good times " for the people, that is, for the workingmen ; and that there is already sufficient wealth in existence in our country to give the working people good times, if it were only rightly distributed.

This, after many years of observation, extending to most of the States of our country, I believe to be a just estimate of our present condition and tendencies. We have a great increase and development of unfavorable and disorganizing forces within our national life, and no corresponding increase of wholesome or vital activities. The influence of the church and of religion upon the morals and conduct of men has greatly declined, and is still declining. There is yet, as I have said, a large amount of moral force and healthful life in the church. Religion is not extinct. But the really significant fact here is that it is constantly losing ground. The empire of religion over human conduct, its power as a conservative moral and social force, is so far lost that some things which are indispensable to the existence of society can no longer be supplied from this source without a great increase of vitality in religion itself. The morality based upon the religion popularly professed has, to a fatal extent, broken down. Multitudes of men who are religious are not honest or trustworthy. They declare themselves fit for heaven, but they will not tell the truth, nor deal justly with their neighbors. The money of widows and orphans placed under their control is not safer than in the hands of highwaymen. There is no article of food, medicine, or traffic which can be profitably adulterated or injuriously manipulated that is not, in most of the great centres of trade, thus corrupted and sold by prominent members of Christian churches. I have made all these statements as colorless as possible, desiring to present a coldly accurate report of the more important facts and tendencies of the life and thought of our country as I have observed them. The evils mentioned are highly complex in character, and are parts of a system over which individuals, as such, have little power. We must take account of them as a wise captain acquaints himself with the position and numbers of a hostile force.

Our situation is the more unfavorable because of the inevitable decline of patriotism among us immediately after the war, — a lowering of national vitality which still affects us seriously. This was largely caused by the utter exhaustion of the faculties of the people ; an incapacity of their powers of brain, nerve, and mind for continned action in the same directions after the fearful tension maintained during the struggle. As all our intellectual and moral activities are correlated with physical forces, this exhaustion was unavoidable, and any great moral effort on the part of the people at the close of the war was next to impossible. This has most probably had something to do with the great indifference in regard to the violation of the laws displayed by local communities. The leading citizens· in many places habitually transgress some laws, finding it convenient or profitable to disregard them. In one of the best towns of an Eastern State the principal property holders and public-spirited citizens met from time to time for some months, last year, to devise measures to repress crime and .immorality, and to promote the order and welfare of the community. The relation of society to pauperism, the sources of vice, the province of legislation, and the duty of good men in relation to such subjects were freely discussed. Two or three gentlemen urged the adoption· of some expression, by these chief men of the place, of their sense of the importance of strict obedience to the laws on the part of all good citizens ; but it was impossible to obtain anything of the kind. I have learned that the same thing has occurred in several other places. Some of this evil may be due to over-legislation ; but, whatever may be the causes, we are becoming a nation of law-breakers. The laws relating to streets, sidewalks, and domestic animals, for instance, and various other minor statutes, are habitually violated in country places by some of the best people. The great number of people from other countries now living in nearly all our towns and villages, and the frequent removals to other places on the part of many citizens, are hindrances to the speedy attainment of a real unity or homogeneous character by the population of our local communities. People will not love their country unless they love the place where they live and endeavor to promote its interests.

It is said that our system of popular education provides sufficient safeguards against the dangers here pointed out. But even if its work were henceforth to be perfect, its operation would necessarily be too slow for some things which our present situation requires. Our school system as it now exists cannot be depended on to remedy or avert the evils which threaten us. Most of the class whose use of prehistoric methods of thought leads them to rely upon instinct and intuition, rather than upon any results of human experience, have enjoyed the opportunities of our schools, and have received, in an average degree, the benefits which our system of education now confers. The people from whom these dangers arise are not stupid or ignorant, nor are their minds inactive. They have been through our schools; they edit newspapers, make our political speeches in all the country places, and represent us in Congress. They are not so much uneducated as miseducated; their faculties are active, particularly of late years, but they are undisciplined and misdirected, and the result of their thinking is largely erroneous. For these difficulties our public school system furnishes no adequate remedy. Two things are especially to be noted in our popular school education : it usually leads to no interest in literature or acquaintance with it, nor to any sense of the value of history for modern men, — a very serious defect; and its most characteristic and general result is a distaste for manual labor. We have some good schools, of course; but great numbers of teachers and principals of our high schools in country places have for several years explicitly taught their pupils, and urged upon parents, the sentiment that in this country education should raise all who obtain it above the necessity of drudgery; that there are better ways of making a living than manual labor " at so much for a day's work," and that these higher ways will be open to those who " get an education."

All this has resulted in a dainty, effeminate, and false view of the world as a place where only uneducated and inferior people need work hard, or engage in toilsome or unattractive employments.

There are two or three small bodies of dissenters from the popular religions whose work is one of the factors of the life of the nation. They have prepared some excellent material for a better state of things. A few cultivated men among them have given the nation the best of its literature. The work of most of the ministers among these dissenters is at present, indeed, rather more literary in its character than is desirable. They do not so much preach as write literary essays. Their position is, however, in large measure, a necessity, and the character of their work up to the present time has been the inevitable product of the most important intellectual and religious movement of the century. But a vital advance ought also now to be inevitable for them. Some of them see the gravity of our national situation and prospects, and are doing all in their power to prepare the people about them for wise and wholesome action and life in the service of the country. Others cherish an urbane philosophical optimism, and smile at the idea of any serious danger to American institutions, political or religious. But these live curiously remote from the common people, or meet them only in the peculiar relations which charity involves. They often know more about other times and lands than our own. Most of them are, like the best men in the pulpits of all the churches, loyally devoted to truth, and eager to be helpful to mankind, but they have to contend at every step against the spirit of the age. The people of this country are — to apply a phrase from M. Raoul Pictet — "prone to value none but paying facts." They know what kind of preaching they want, and they intend to have it. If one minister does not supply it, they employ another. It is expected that ministers will preach on national interests or morals on Thanksgiving Day and on the Fourth of July; but as things are now few congregations would listen, without serious dissatisfaction, to any thorough or adequate treatment of the subjects which are most important and vital for us as a nation. After a few such discourses there would be an imperative demand for sermons of the usual type. The good people in the churches are weary and careworn when Sunday comes, and wish to be comforted, soothed, and entertained by the preaching. And in this commercial age they will not " pay " for preaching which does not suit them. So there are many men whose religious teaching is of the wisest who have much difficulty to live, and who are entirely unable to equip themselves as they should for their work. If there is any new development of moral forces or increase of religious vitality in our time, these small companies of dissenters from the popular religion will have a close and vital connection with it, though not in sectarian ways.

As to that numerous class of people who insist that Christianity is itself exhausted and outgrown, and that we have already reached something better, they have not developed anything that can help us in our present needs. They do something in opposing the superstitions and absurdities of some church people, but thus far their criticism has been narrow, sectarian, and unpractical. The priests of the Roman Catholic Church occupy a position of great importance in relation to the new conditions and tendencies of our national life. Although many of them are rather churchmen than American citizens, their influence is likely to be, on the whole, rather helpful than otherwise. They do a vast deal of good work upon very difficult material. Their course should be critically observed, but they deserve far more sympathy and recognition than they receive. Their teaching forbids consultation of the spirits of the dead, and membership in secret societies. This last requirement will keep many voters out of the movement for the inflation and debasement of the national currency, as the leaders of that enterprise make great use of the machinery of secret societies.

What then can be done? Is our condition hopeless? By no means. Are we to wait, as some people urge, until these errors and delusions have spent their force? They do not tend to exhaust themselves. They belong naturally to human beings in the stages of development to which those who are affected by them have attained. They have no self-limiting quality, but have abundant power to reproduce and extend themselves. Are we to depend chiefly upon force, as employed in the repression and punishment of riotous proceedings and crimes against property, as the best means for the protection of society and the maintenance of civilization? No. It is true that all positive law rests upon force in the last analysis, and it is often conservative and merciful to enforce obedience to law at whatever cost. But the value and permanence of property, and the vitality of other elements of civilization, depend upon settled, orderly, and peaceful conditions of society. If the evil tendencies I have described are not checked, if we are to live in a state of constant apprehension of riots and conflagrations, or if we rely chiefly upon armed force to prevent such outbreaks, our legislation will necessarily be unwholesomely affected to such an extent, and the business and industries of our country so disturbed and depressed, that our national condition would have to be regarded as little better than the real failure of our institutions. Other dangers than that of the pillage and destruction of our cities by armed mobs may be serious enough to tax the vital resources of the nation to the utmost. We must somehow eliminate and transmute a large proportion of this dangerous and inflammable material, and we must greatly increase the healthful forces in the life of the nation.

The evil of false and foolish teaching can be adequately resisted only by true teaching and wise action. It is said that persons who hold the sentiments and cherish the aims here depicted are beyond the reach of argument or reason. That is true of many, probably of all, the teachers and leaders of this class. But it is not true, as yet, of the multitude from whom this class is being constantly recruited. It is not yet true of the young people who are coming up, year by year, to take their places in those ranks. The ideas and impulses which tend to disorder and disintegration, when they have taken possession of the minds of men, do indeed constitute a craze, an epidemic hallucination or contagion of unreason and folly. This conception has been well developed, and it gives us one of the most acute and discriminating notions of our time. It is the key to many things otherwise inexplicable in history. But the circumstances, influences, and conditions which predispose or prepare men for the reception and development of the germs of this contagion have not been sufficiently considered. Here is a fact of great interest for us. The number of those who cannot be influenced by argument or any direct intellectual appeal is increasing from month to month, and it is recruited from classes who are still accessible, who could be guided if there were anybody to guide them ; who could be taught and enlightened if the right means were used; who might be confirmed and established in their now wavering allegiance to truth, justice, and sound reason. There is a vast field and opportunity for successful work in this direction. It waits only the awakening of the cultivated.classes to the perils, needs, and duties of the hour.

But the people who cannot be influenced by argument are by no means in a state so hopeless as most of our teachers believe. The truth is that comparatively few men are controlled or guided so much by argument and reason as by the earnestness, the convictions, and the confident activity of those who have made up their minds, and are heartily interested in a definite object. And especially are men influenced and attracted by the volume and mass of the teaching and movements around them. They are swayed and decided by the continuity of attack, by the cumulative force of the constant iteration of the same idea in varying forms. These things depend upon natural laws, and the apostles of disorder are working in accordance with these laws, which are always potent in the propagation of feelings, opinions, and convictions. These laws are not partial to falsehood and folly. They lend themselves as readily and efficiently to the dissemination of truth and good sense.

But there is a kind of fetich worship of the power of ideas which prevails among our cultivated people, which leads them to think that when they have demonstrated the excellence and superiority of certain principles, by means of a paper in a review, or an essay at a meeting of ministers, their work is done, and that the conquest of the world by their opinions is only a matter of time; and so they turn away, serenely triumphant, to await the happy consummation. But ideas have little practical efficiency until they are incarnated, so to speak, — made alive and personal in men and women; until a few people, at least, care a great deal about them, and feel a resistless impulse to their propagation. This impulse is precisely what our cultivated people do not feel in regard to any ideas whatever. Propagandism of any kind repels them. This is the weakness of our nation to-day, and the source of its greatest danger. The people who believe in civilization are giving away the victory to their wild antagonists by their own inaction, a delusion of their culture which makes them disdain to learn the use of new weapons and methods. Culture itself is not yet in this country vital or dynamic. It lacks the impulse and virility necessary for its own propagation. It is too dainty for a land like ours, and is inclined to be discouraged about the masses, or else to trust everything to " the resistless operation of the laws of progress." Now that is a phrase merely. Many persons feel soothed and strengthened when they hear it, but it does not mean much. If anything is done for the improvement of life and its conditions in this country we must begin, and must be prepared for a large and persistent expenditure of time, of thought, and of personal effort; with the usual accompaniments of partial failure, of the incompetence of some of the agents, and of much unrecognized and unhonored toil. Direct endeavor for the elevation of any class is less repulsive after we have heartily engaged in it. However distasteful it may be, it is the condition of our success, and cannot be safely postponed to a more favorable time. Such work is not so hopeless as some would have us believe. Two fluids may be kept permanently apart by a thin membrane if both are at rest; but if one is set in motion the other will pass through the intervening wall and join in the movement. When there is a vital advance on the part of our cultivated people new motions will be set up and new centres of force developed in the life of the nation at large. The working people will exert themselves for their own improvement if we begin ; they are not likely to do so otherwise.

We shall wholly fail if we think we can improve society, or any portion of it, by any plan which does not require improvement on the part of the more fortunate and cultivated classes. Much of their culture is superficial and unpractical, consisting rather of unrelated fragments of thought, and vague impressions concerning what is supposed to be known, than of real knowledge resulting from the ordered activity of a disciplined intelligence. We need a better culture for our teachers and leaders ; not merely more of the same kind they now possess, but culture of a higher order. It will not do to confine our interest or efforts to the lower strata. We must learn how to solve such problems as pauperism, or poor-relief, and prison management; but woe to our nation if we expend all our vitality upon them. We must do this and have strength for higher interests and more constructive work. The lower classes are now educating us. A necessary tendency and peril of democracy, of a universal suffrage arrangement of society, is a general mediocrity, the adoption of low standards, a halting of the army of civilization while we wait for the camp-followers to come up. Let us distribute rations among these if that is best. But their place is not in front, and the head of the column must move on. We must open the way ahead, and not merely fortify the rear of our position.

The people who believe in culture, in property, and in order, that is in civilization, must establish the necessary agencies for the diffusion of a new culture. Capital must protect itself by organized activities for a new object, — the education of the people. Those who possess property, and those who value it as one of the great forces and supports of civilization, will be obliged to learn that legislation, even if the laws are properly enforced, is not an adequate means for the protection of property and the repression of the disorderly and destructive elements in our society. Legislation itself is fast becoming a weapon in the hands of the hostile forces; and even if it were always the

work of wise men it is only one factor of civilization, and would not give us security without a
great advance in the culture and character of the
people. Our present conditions cannot be permanent. If they are not improved they will soon
grow worse. The evils which threaten us must
be studied and understood, and then dealt with
rationally, and some of their sources must be
cut off.

The present slovenly and miserably inefficient
procedure in dealing with tramps, vagrants, and
people destitute of food and employment must be
changed by taking some unit of territory, a town-
ship, ward, or county, and then confining all who
need relief to the district in which they belong or
may be found. Labor which will yield them food,
not wages, should be provided, and all persons
supplied with food should be compelled to work.
As it is now, a vast army marches around the
land, refusing all work, and receiving far more
food and money than would be necessary to maintain it if the business were organized on business
principles. Our country roads are unsafe for
women, and our cities swarm with stalwart beg-
gars who threaten when their demands are not
satisfied.

A friend of mine, a missionary in one of our
largest cities, last winter preached in a large hall
on Sunday evenings, and spent some hours each
Saturday night in the streets and alleys of that
vicinity. To all who asked for money to procure

something to eat or a place to sleep he gave food (when they would take it; many would accept nothing but money), and secured for them a comfortable lodging. Then, giving each applicant a card, with time and place of services for the next evening, he invited him to attend the meeting, and promised him supper and lodging for Sunday night also. More than a hundred men were thus kindly treated, but not one of them ever came to the Sunday evening meeting. My friend said that of the whole number there was but one who seemed to be really hungry.

But there are more types than one, and we must not estimate the situation by one such report alone. During the last few years I have myself seen the wives and children of workingmen in country towns die of inanition, after having long subsisted on a little Indian meal. Discovery came too late. These people met their fate silently. They were known to be poor and out of work, and "they would not beg." Many persons have died in some regions of our country, during the last three years, from disease induced by insufficient nourishment, and many invalids among the poor have succumbed to the effects of scant and unsuitable food. A young girl, whose wages as a servant had procured a bare subsistence for her mother and three small children, lost her place recently by the death of her mistress. Unable to find employment, and distracted by the hunger of the children, she applied to a friend of mine for advice. Said she, " Mrs. ———, what is the right way for people to live when they can get nothing to eat?" On behalf of her inarticulate class I repeat her question. As teachers of the poor we should be prepared to offer them a philosophy of life suited to their circumstances. We say truly that some of their theories are wild, and their aims fatal to their own interests. But we must give voice to the plea which they ought to make, and ourselves champion the aims which would be wise and right for them. Again the question, What are they? If we should have for several years a succession of abundant crops, the pressure and urgency of some of our dangers would be lessened. If, on the other hand, we have unfavorable seasons and continued. industrial depression, these difficulties would be aggravated. It is not wise to depend for safety upon chances which are in no degree under our control.

I am aware that my arraignment of the inadequacy of the means now being used requires some suggestion of more vigorous methods of action for our national regeneration, or for a decided increase of healthful activities in the intellectual and moral life of our country. A society with a plan or method of work resembling that of the New England Loyal Publication Society, which did so much to reinforce the national sentiment during our civil war, could now render quite as efficient service. Few people, except newspaper men, know to what extent most newspapers out of the cities are made up, or supplied with matter, by the mere accident of proximity, or readiness to the editor's scissors, of articles of suitable length, already printed, so that they can be rapidly glanced over and conveniently transferred to his paper. I would have a society or arrangement of some kind for printing and sending to the country newspapers everywhere a series of broadsides or sheets filled with short articles, plainly written, direct and spirited in style, without eloquence or bookishness, and with few figures of speech; setting forth and repeating in ever-varying forms the few great simple truths and facts which explain our present national condition, especially in connection with such subjects as debt, paper money, resumption of specie payments, and the relation of individual habits and expenditures to national welfare.

We need also the publication of a small, low-priced newspaper, for circulation in all parts of the country; to be printed in the best style, giving a good digest of the most important news; to be dedicated to the propagation and definite teaching of strict honesty, wise economy, fraternal self-denial and a religious devotion to our country, and the interests of a nobler civilization than we have yet attained; a paper for the people, which shall have for its aim the development of a national spirit and temper, of a practical, capable, and wholesome nature, leading men away from empty theories of millennial progress and attainments to

manly self-reliance and intelligent recognition of
the real conditions of human life in this world ; a
paper, in short, which shall represent and propagate principles, sentiments, and activities ·in accord with the central ideas of this article.

We need some small books on subjects connected with political economy, which shall teach
what is known, however little that may prove to
be, and not merely perplex the brains of workingmen by reporting the speculations of all the
schools. We need a great deal of elementary
teaching, and should have books written for plain
people, by authors who can drive straight at the
mark and stop when they have done.

The persuasive power of public speaking, lect-
uring, and preaching is of course indispensable.
It should be employed in the education of the
people as fast as honest men who have a real
grasp upon these principles can be found to speak
clearly and usefully. People everywhere who per-
ceive these needs should meet, confer with each
other, and begin to work.

The central or fundamental philosophical truth
which underlies the mental and moral culture
which the age requires is the truth of the moral
order of the universe. Human life belongs to an
actual order, — a cosmos, not a chaos ; and this
order is a moral order, and tends to and prefers
truth, justice, and righteousness. The opposite
error, which has misled a large portion of American society, is the opinion that the moral order to

which man's life belongs is subjective only; that nothing is true or right in itself, but only as it seems so to us; that there is no real standard of human conduct, only a conventional one; and that if men would generally agree to it the relations and nature of right and wrong might be reversed.   This is what is really fatal in unbelief in our time, — not the rejection of the creed of my church or yours, but the loss of the perception and assurance of the truth that the laws of nature and the inevitable working of the forces of the universe are hostile to falsehood and injustice; that extreme individualism is now abnormal and self-destructive; and that fraternal or social justice is provided for and required by the constitution of things, by the laws of an order which man did not make and cannot change.   There is a great deal to be said on the other side.   If there were not, we should have no difficulties or problems, and no such arduous task before us here in the education of the people and their emancipation from error and folly.

We must insist on the necessity of sincerity and of knowledge on the part of religious teachers. We need the development of a religion for this world, for the needs and duties of life here. Strictly speaking we have no knowledge of another world or a future life. We may believe profoundly, but we do not know. Belief, trust, and faith are also, as truly as knowledge, great dynamic forces in human life, and have a value of their own. We must have a religion and moral philosophy which will inspire patriotism, and hold us strenuously to the work of making this country a clean, orderly, and wholesome dwelling-place, school, and home for human beings. The religious people and the scientific people are alike foolish and blind when they do not see their equal need of each other as allies against the assault of forces which are equally hostile to both. All who will work for the health of the nation must be welcomed and encouraged. What is good and effective in the church and its teaching will disentangle itself somewhat from that which is lifeless and worldly, if there is anywhere a distinct forward movement. The secular press should criticise frankly the preaching of the day, in so far as it concerns morality and national interests, and we must all expect the most rigid scrutiny of what we teach. We must hasten the introduction into religious speech (varying a little Professor Clarke Maxwell's expression) " of words and phrases consistent with true ideas about nature, instead of others implying false ideas."

The people who believe that the utilitarian doctrines provide a sufficient basis for morality should feel an imperative requirement, in the circumstances of our country, for the development of those doctrines. So far as they are capable of becoming a religious inspiration and motive for men, they should be made available to the utmost possible extent. They do not yet constitute a religion, except perhaps to a few persons, who represent in a rare degree what is best and highest in American civilization. We need work, just here, by a master's hand, in setting forth the character, meaning, scope, and practical requirements of the utilitarian doctrines in relation to the circumstances and conditions of life in this country to-day. What does utilitarianism teach, and why should men regard and obey it?

A change in the reading of the people is necessary, if we are to improve the national life. Men who could really teach English literature, and show people how to read and understand it, so as to receive culture from it, would be among the most valuable missionaries of the new order of things. If there are such men it would be profitable to employ them.

Men of property or wealth, capitalists, and people of culture who understand the value of property in civilization must accept a great and direct responsibility in regard to all matters pertaining to the moral education of the people. Their course will decide what our national condition shall be for some time to come. We have been too much inclined to hold a few half-starved clergymen chiefly responsible for the moral culture of the masses. There is no good reason for making self-sacrifice and unrecompensed labor for such objects the business of ministers exclusively.

People will say, All this will require a great deal of money. True; but it will save much more. If the future of this country is to be evolved from the elements and tendencies of the present, then, unless something like what is here outlined is undertaken and carried forward, the loss of property (not to speak of moral losses) will be greater than the amount of money that would be required for an educational enterprise on a larger scale than any the past has known. We ought to expend a million of dollars in this work during the next three years, as a beginning. It would be a most profitable business enterprise, — considered merely as an investment of money, — on account of the pecuniary losses which it would prevent.

I observe much complaint lately of the difficulties involved in universal suffrage. They are doubtless great. If the world were wholly different we might do fine things. But we must have methods that can be used as things are, — to begin with, at least. The age is probably the most unteachable since the Revival of Learning. But we can work to-day only where we are. We are shut up to this universal suffrage organization of society, and must find out how to make it serve the ends for which society exists. The franchise is not likely to be narrowed greatly in our time. If America were a jungle of human tigers, still it is our country and the country of our children, and its people, however undeveloped and intractable, are our neighbors, brethren, and fellow-citizens. We must live in some relations with them, and to make these relations orderly, beneficent, and just is worth all it can cost. The union of the States is geographical, official, and mechanical; the unity of the people must be vital, organie, and spiritual. Such unity is not yet actual, only potential.

THE NATIONALS, THEIR ORIGIN AND THEIR AIMS.

THE history of the National Party begins with the financial legislation of our civil war. The equipment of the Union soldiery, and other preparations for national defense, required the expenditure of vast sums beyond what the national treasury could supply. The government issued printed notes — promises to pay — to the amount of many millions of dollars, enacting that these notes should be regarded and used as a legal tender in all the ordinary business of the people, but excepting from this provision certain dues and payments of the government for which coin was required. As the war assumed greater proportions the necessary purchases became enormous in extent, and the remarkable discovery was made that everybody might easily become rich by selling goods to the government at prices many times greater than their real value. It was easy to print the paper promises to pay, and the government scattered them with lavish hand among the people. There was an unexampled expansion and activity in all kinds of business. Everybody could obtain employment at high wages. There was a new market for everything, and the demand seemed un-

limited. Men counted their new wealth by hundreds of thousands and millions. It consisted of
the evidences of the government's indebtedness,
that is, of their own. The result of the war was
for some time uncertain. No day had been fixed
for the payment of the legal-tender notes, and
their purchasing power declined as the numbers
issued were multiplied. The war ended. The
government went out of business, that is, it was
no longer a purchaser to any great extent; the
new market was closed. Most of the people of
the country had been really in the employ of the
government during the war, nearly all traders and
speculators receiving lavish salaries in the excessive profits of their business. Now everybody was
discharged. The hasty, desperate, make-shift
financial legislation at the beginning of the war
had produced a great " expansion of the currency," filling the hands of the people everywhere with the new paper money. But the vast
amount in circulation had to be reduced; some
arrangement for complying with the promise to
pay (printed on the face of every note) had to be
adopted, or the notes would soon be worthless.
Then came the contraction of the currency by the
retirement of some of the legal-tender notes. The
new taxes were a great burden; the best investments produced but small profits; and we were
rudely awakened from splendid dreams of increasing prosperity to distasteful economies and comparative poverty. The nation began, in great

depression and bewilderment, the payment of its
tremendous war debt. The people had generally
used the government's promises to pay as real
money, vaguely considering the new paper cur-
reney as an addition to the actual wealth of the
country, without fully realizing that the people
had to pay the debt of the nation. There were
multitudes who did not understand why the vast
expansion of business and industry should be temporary ; why the " prosperity of the war-time "
should not continue forever. There was no adequate effort to teach them. They had been in-
credulous when the first signs of the inevitable
decline and collapse appeared. They had lost the
habit of hard labor, and when they found that the
days of contracts and jobs, and of easy, profuse
living were past they were profoundly dissatisfied.
In that dissatisfaction was the origin of the discontent, the grievances, hopes, and purposes of the people who constitute the mass of the national party
of to-day. The stream has received some important
tributaries in later times, but this was its source.

It took some little time to formulate the new
feeling. But it was soon discovered that when
the paper money was abundant the country was
prosperous, and that the first contraction of the
currency and the decline in business were coinci-
dent in time, and were therefore related to each
other as cause and effect. It was affirmed that if
the paper money had been made a full legal tender, that is, if it had been received by the gov-

ernment for all dues and used in payment of all
claims, it would always have been equal to gold in
value or purchasing power. The legislation providing that coin should be used in the payment of
duties, and of the interest on national bonds, was
denounced as injurious to the people, as was also
the act establishing national banks. A feeling of
opposition to the payment of debts which were
incurred during the period of the inflation of the
currency became very strong, especially in the
West. The continued and increasing depression
of business and of industry has deepened and
strengthened these tendencies, and the time has
been in many ways propitious for their growth.

A history of the paper-money delusion from its
origin, through the various stages of its influence
upon both the great political parties of the country, with a careful study of their platforms and of
the utterances of their leading men upon financial
subjects during the last seventeen years, including a review of the development of allied influences and of the effect of all these tendencies
upon the national thought and life, would be a
most instructive and valuable work, but it must
be left to other hands. What is here undertaken
is a presentation or report of the specific opinions,
grievances, illusions, hopes, and purposes of the
people who are identified with the national party.
In making this report I have as far as possible
used the exact words of my neighbors and fellow-
citizens who hold these opinions ; and when ver-

bal changes were necessary I have endeavored to preserve their thoughts and ideas with scrupulous accuracy. No part of the materials for this report is taken from newspapers or printed documents, or from public addresses. During the last few weeks I have had very full and satisfactory conversations with thirty-four workingmen who are earnest adherents of the new national party. The number includes residents of three different States, Pennsylvania, New York, and New Jersey. I am personally acquainted with all of them. They are natives of this country, and men of good repute for honesty and general morality. Most of them are poor, and they all work with their hands. They have what is usually called in this country a good common-school education, and most of them have more than this. More than half have been teachers. They are of all ages, from thirty-two to fifty-seven. What is here presented was expressed in answer to my questions on all the subjects brought forward. In every instance I received the utmost courtesy, with permission to communicate to the public the information thus given to me. I used a note-book and pencil as we talked, recording as fully as possible what was said, often repeating the questions and reading my memoranda to my neighbor for his approval. On most essential points there was substantial agreement among all these men, but I have noted some differences of individual opinion and aim. Here are the notes : —

BANKS AND BANKING.

" The national party is the result of a great uprising of the people. The industrial classes are
becoming enlightened. It is a movement from
the bottom of society. We have no leaders as
yet, and it is probably better so. The movement
may develop leaders by and by. It has grown
thus far by talks between neighbors, and by the
influence of newspapers and printed documents.
We have one weekly paper, with a circulation of
six hundred and fifty thousand copies, and an increase each week of twenty thousand. We are
organizing in every school district in many States,
and in every ward of the cities. We wish to abolish the national banks. All the commercial pan-
ics in our history have been caused largely by the
system of state and national banking. The bankers deposit one hundred thousand dollars at Washington, and the government gives them back
ninety thousand dollars in bank-notes for the bare
cost of printing, say one per cent. The government pays them six per cent. on the one hundred
thousand dollars. Then they have ninety thousand dollars to loan at the legal rate of interest,
and as much more as they can get. They receive
from twenty-five to fifty per cent., and sometimes
one hundred per cent., per annum on their original investment. We want absolute money, not a
promise to pay; would have gold, silver, and
paper all issued directly by the government, with-

out the intervention of any banking corporation; the legend to be, *This is a Dollar* (or whatever the amount may be), making it a legal tender in payment of all dues and claims whatever. Of course we shall need new legislation for such a currency. This national absolute money would buy anything in any market of the world with one fourth or one half of one per cent. discount in exchange. There are about two thousand national banks, and they now have a surplus fund of sixteen hundred millions of dollars. The bankers have received so much interest that nearly all existing deposits are clear profit; that is, they have cost them nothing. The masses of mankind are trodden under foot and enslaved by a vicious financial system, and we are tending to the low conditions of the older nations. Combinations of capitalists and unfavorable legislation crush the la borer. The beginning of these evils is the fallacy of a gold basis. There is not enough gold for all the world's money; if there were it would be all right. Banks may have done good in early times in the West, but our advanced civilization requires a currency not based upon coin. We favor the immediate repeal of the resumption act. With national absolute money no resumption of specie payments would be required. The bullionists favor resumption and contraction; they bring gold to par by their designing manipulations. It is no advantage to the people to have gold at par. European capitalists have influenced the financial legislation of our country a great deal. Their design is to break up our republican government. We have positive proof that a man came over from England with half a million of money to oppose the passage of the silver bill; but he found that it would do no good. History shows that no country has ever prospered on a coin basis."

FRIENDS AND FOES.

" We have some of the most talented men in political economy with us, but not many. Professioual men, such as clergymen, are not enough interested in these matters to investigate the real condition of the laboring classes and their needs. The masses are sufficiently intelligent and morally educated to see that class legislation or any injustice would be fatal to themselves. The mass of mankind have common sense. It requires no special talent for investigation to enable men to understand what is necessary for their own interests in such matters. When members of Congress begin to legislate in favor of the moneyed class their constituents ought to be able to say, Stop! that is not what you were employed to do. Legislators should execute the wishes of the people who elect them. We favor shortening the hours of labor. Political economists say that four hours a day would probably be adequate to maintain all mankind in comfort, and give them some of the luxuries of life, providing richly for the helpless."

INTERNAL IMPROVEMENTS.

" We would have the government begin immediately the construction of extensive works of internal improvement. The Erie Canal should be enlarged to a ship canal sufficient for vessels of two thousand tons burden. A canal of the same capacity should be constructed across the State of Michigan, and another across Northern Florida."

MONEY AND BONDS.

" I do not undertake to speak for the national party ; there are differences of opinion on many points among those who are working together in this movement. I would not permit individuals or corporations to engage in any kind of banking enterprise ; not even for exchange, or to receive deposits. All such business should be conducted by the government. The value of gold and silver coin is in the government stamp upon it, and not in the intrinsic worth of the metal. Money should be made of material which has no intrinsic value. The contraction of the currency is the greatest cause of the prostration of industry. The national bonds are a fraud upon the people, and Rothschild knew it at first. The 5–20 bonds were originally to be paid in greenbacks, and only their interest in coin, but by a change in legislation the principal was afterwards required to be paid in coin. The bonds cost holders thirty-five cents on the dollar in gold, and by laws contracting the currency the bonds have been made worth more than gold. The holders have already received more than the cost of the bonds, and still hold them."

GOVERNMENTAL OWNERSHIP.

" The government is a great commune. All railroads, canals, and means of commercial transportation, and all mines and land, should belong to the government. There should be no individual ownership in land, but only of improvements. There should be no law for the collection of interest. The amount of money in circulation should be increased by the government issuing as much absolute money as is needed by the people, and paying it out for all government expenses, and for the wages of laborers employed on public works. Resumption is a speculation of the capitalists. There is no need of specie payments. The people have not asked for the measure ; it is forced upon them. The resumption act should be immediately repealed. All history shows that in order to maintain specie payments we must have more specie than paper money. There should be enough money to give the people a sufficient medium of exchange. We should pay the bonds in greenbacks as far as possible. If the legislation changing the nature of the bonds and requiring their payment in coin was right, then counter-legislation would be."

PROHIBITION OF LARGE FORTUNES.

" All officers should be elected by the people directly, and no law should take effect until it has been submitted to the people and been approved by them. We should have whatever legislation is necessary for imposing an income tax graduated so as not to touch small incomes, to grow heavier for larger fortunes, and to be made absolutely prohibitive for accumulations beyond a certain limit. No man should be permitted to hold more land than he uses, and the acquisition of great fortunes should be made impossible. One of our greatest dangers is the power of a landed aristocracy."

REPRESENTATION OF CLASSES.

" All classes should be represented in our national legislature in proportion to their numbers. Legislation by lawyers is always devoted to the interests of their own class. The people of culture in this country underestimate the intelligence of the masses. Capitalists could buy workingmen's votes as easily as they now buy those of lawyers: we shall have to depend largely upon the effect of the opposition between different classes for checking any tendency to excess, injustice, or corruption. Capitalists feel like kings and aristocrats, and regard the workingmen as their slaves. If these evils cannot be removed by legislation, it will be done in some other way. If people dread war or mob-law, they should help the workingmen overthrow the money power. Capitalists dread nothing so much as the uprising of the masses. We have two thousand bankers representing two billions of capital."

CULTIVATED PEOPLE ANTAGONISTIC.

" The college men are not in the national movement, rnd usually misunderstand it entirely. Their education destroys natural perception and judgment; so that cultivated people are one-sided, and their judgment is often inferior to that of the working people. History shows that all through the ages the evolution of new ideas has come from the lower classes, the uneducated. We should naturally look outside of the professions for the leaders of a new movement. Professional men are usually against us. The uneducated are more accessible, more easily influenced, than the educated. Cultured people have made up their minds, and are hard to move. There should be a check upon Chinese immigration. Our civilization cannot maintain itself in contact with Chinese civilization. That will survive where ours cannot, and if we live together we shall have to conform to their civilization."

MONEY AND CONSTITUTIONS.

" For three hundred years the progress of civilized nations has been in the direction of absolute money. Money should be composed of some material that is not in itself precious or commercially valuable. Constitutional provisions are of little importance compared with the direct expression of the will of the people. The real law is not written or printed. Popular feeling is really the law rather any statute."

HAPPINESS AND LOST LUGGAGE.

"Happiness is the legal tender of the soul. Four hours a day is enough for anybody to work, but people should work every day. To rest on Sunday, or one day each week, is wrong. Government should own and operate the railroads of the country. We could then recover the value of trunks if they were lost in transportation. Now it is often difficult or impossible. Burning up the money when it was called in to contract the currency, instead of sending it out again to circulate among the people, is the real cause of the distress of the country. No lawyer should be elected to a a place in any legislative body."

HELP FROM THE SPIRIT WORLD.

"We might obtain much help from the spirit world. There is a Congress there of all our great statesmen, who have passed away. They see the future and know the motives of men, and they preside over the affairs of our country. They have already had much to do with our national affairs. The spirit of Washington once sent a medium to Lincoln with military plans which the president executed. It would be wise to put the management of the Indians wholly under the direction of the spirits. We might obtain very great aid from the spirit world in regard to all difficult questions connected with the science of government. The national movement is likely to go farther than most people foresee."

GOVERNMENTAL PAWNBROKING.

" The government might loan money to the people to the extent of half the value of goods deposited in government warehouses (appraised by competent men, and to be held until redeemed). We should use gold, silver, and paper, till the metals naturally drop out of circulation. Paper money will soon expel gold and silver money from the country. Government should not require more than three per cent. interest on loans to the people; many of the nationals would have interest prohibited by a provision in the Constitution of the country."

THE MONEY POWER TO BE BROKEN DOWN.

" The object of the greenback party is to break down the money power, politically, commercially, and industrially. The government should build a railroad from Norfolk, Virginia, to California, and should take possession of all railroads, canals, and telegraphs. All should be operated at cost, — without profit. We make no account of constitutional difficulties in the way of these things, or of what the Constitution forbids or allows. It is not best to make many constitutional provisions. Constitutions are things to have discussions about, and to form the subject of points of order in debate, rather than for practical efficiency or obligation. They should be composed, as nearly as may be, of undoubted basic principles. These objects should be attained either by coöperation or by communal organization. The greenback system tends to a national communal organization or association as to banking, railroad transportation, and similar branches of business."

FREE LAND.

" Air, earth, and water should be free to all. A man may own improvements, but not the land. We should make the taxes on large accumulations of landed property so high that the owners cannot pay them, and so cannot keep the land. Land in its natural, original, and unimproved condition is not rightly to be regarded as property. Its use should be subject to control by the government."

ORIGIN AND ORGANIZATION.

" The national party includes the greenback movement, which originated in the dissatisfaction of the people with the contraction of the currency after the war, and the other gold-basis legislation of that period; the labor movement is another branch of the party. The growth of our cause has also been largely stimulated and assisted by the influence of the internationals and of the German socialists. Our present programme is not final or complete. The first object is to change the nature of the currency and abolish the banks. Then comes the seizure by labor of its rightful empire, and government ownership of railroads and other means of transportation and commerce; it is not yet certain which of these will come first. The granger movement has done much to prepare material for the national party, and trades-unions and other secret organizations have had a large share in developing it; they are now among the most efficient agencies for the propagation of our principles and the extension of our power. It is believed that fifteen hundred thousand voters belong to secret labor organizations in this country, but it is impossible to be certain of the numbers. In every place in which the nationals have been successful in elections, their strength has come from these secret labor organizations."

TERMS OF OFFICE.

"Nobody should hold office longer than one year, except the president and members of Congress. They might be elected for two years, and they should all go out together, so as to have all new men after each election."

CONTINUOUS ELECTIONS.

"I would have a continuous election. The polls should be kept open all the time, so that whenever a citizen desires he can go and change his vote and give it to a new man. Then whenever a majority of all the voters of a district or State has pronounced in favor of a new representative, the old one should give place. If the people are dissatisfied with a representative in three weeks after he is chosen, they have a right to dismiss him and elect another."

REDUCED HOURS OF LABOR.

" Whenever the hours of labor have been reduced, or the pay of workingmen increased, there has been an increase of intelligence and morality, and a diminution of intemperance and crime."

BONDS.

" The 5–20 bonds, of which seven or eight hundred millions are still out, were originally to be paid in greenbacks; the law requiring their payment in coin should be repealed. We should have legislation making all bonds payable in greenbacks. All bonds that are to be paid in gold were made so by fraud."

NEW ISSUE OF CURRENCY.

" An issue of two thousand millions of the new currency (absolute money) would probably not depreciate the currency more than thirty per cent."

GOVERNMENTAL EDUCATION.

"We favor education by the state; it should be industrial and compulsory, allowing for differenccs in character and circumstances. The problems or examples in school-books should be of an industrial and not of a commercial nature."

LABOR BUREAUS.

" The government should establish a labor bureau in each State, and one for the nation, to collect industrial statistics, and, in time, to regulate the agricultural production of the country, — to determine, for instance, how many sweet potatoes would probably be needed each year, so that the market might not be oversupplied."

ASSOCIATIONS.

" The people will form associations everywhere. When we have an international government or superintendency, as we must have with international money, this will lead to the gradual disuse or comparative abolition of nationalities, and the association of the people of the whole world for the government of the whole world."

CATHOLIC NATIONALS.

" We think the national movement, so far as it tends to association, is opposed to the influence of the clergy. We have a strong following among the Catholics, and thousands of them are in the secret labor societies."

ABSOLUTE MONEY.

" United States bonds were at first to be paid in legal-tender notes ; a clique of the moneyed men

got together and changed the language so as to require coin, and then demonetized silver. After
that the bankers got control of Congress, and
enacted that the legal-tender notes should not be
received for duties. If the government had received the paper money for all dues it would always have been equal to gold. It is said that
absolute money would not be received in Europe;
we are not making a currency for Europe, but for
our own country. Gold and silver for money are
relics of heathenism. Paper money would naturally expel coin from circulation. We should repeal all laws requiring bonds to be paid in gold.
The bonds were all bought at greenback values.
One thousand dollars in gold bought two thousand five hundred dollars in greenbacks, and that
bought two thousand five hundred dollars in United
States bonds."

TRAMPS.

" The government should employ many of the
tramps, and should engage in the construction of
extensive public works for the relief of the unemployed. All wages should be paid by the hour."

GOVERNMENTAL BANKING AND EMPLOYMENT.

" The government should establish post-office
savings banks, and should pay interest at a rate
not above that of the annual increase of the wealth
of the country, now about three and a half per
cent. per annum. The government ought to be
the employer of the people if the government is

honestly and judiciously administered ; and it is more likely to be so administered under this system than any other.   Of course, if the government takes possession of the railroads it would naturally manufacture its own engines, cars, rails, and equipments generally, and the nation would become a vast coöperative association."

THE PEOPLE ALL-WISE.

" The selfishness of the people will teach them to be just and wise.   They are too intelligent to commit any excesses.   They will lay politicians on the shelf, and take new men.   No capitalist or banker should be nominated for any office whatever by the nationals."

" No doubt there will be excesses of various kinds, and measures of retaliation, when the workingmen obtain control of the government.   That will be only human nature. . There is a considerable proportion of low and brutal material in the national party, but we are not responsible for that. The same men belonged to the other two parties before they joined us, and they are no worse now than when they voted with our opponents."

SOCIETY TO BE CHANGED.

" None of us can speak for the party.   We can only tell you what we think would be best, what we believe in, and what we would do if we could. If we succeed, the general structure of society will be modified in important respects, and religion and morality will no doubt be affected by changes so vital, but in what way, or to what extent, nobody can now foresee."

MORALITY AND RELIGION.

"It is not likely that the organization of society will be affected in any serious way by the changes we propose to make. Morality and religion under the new order of things will be about what they are now."

PROTECTION.

"We favor protection and oppose free trade. We would admit raw materials (such as are not produced in this country) free of duty, but would tax imported manufactured goods."

THE SENATE USELESS.

"The workingmen should direct their efforts to securing an adequate representation, by members of their own class, in the national house of representatives. The senate is of little consequence, and might well be abolished."

It remains for me to add a few facts not included in the conversations thus reported. It was made plain to each of these workingmen that it was not confidential information in regard to the plans of the national party which I sought, but his own estimate of the causes of the movement and of the grievances of the people, and his own opinion and hopes in regard to desirable changes;

and that I sought such information with the purpose to make it public, and thus report as accurately as possible the thought, sentiment, and aims of the masses, the working people.

More than two thirds of the whole number of these workingmen favor protection in some form for American industry ; but some half dozen believe in free trade.

None of these men are Catholics. All of them hold what are called advanced or liberal views of religious or theological subjects, and a few are atheists. Eighteen of the number believe that the spirit world has inspired the new political discontent, and that the national party is constantly aided and reinforced from " the superior spheres." I have myself observed that many mediums and trance-speakers are among the most popular and influential orators now employed in propagating the sentiments of the new party.

In connection with this movement women are engaging in politics more directly and effectively than ever before. Many of them are traveling through the country, speaking on political and social subjects, and their oratory often influences voters as much as that of the men on the same platform. The women have political clubs which meet regularly for discussing the questions of the time.

The thirty-four workingmen with whom I thus conversed are, I think, quite as intelligent as the better class of voters in either of the other two parties. They are well-educated men, according to the popular American standard and idea of education: that is, they are all ready talkers; most of them could make nearly as good speeches as an average congressman; and they have a great deal of such information as is to be obtained from scraps and items in newspapers. They are " up with the times," to use a phrase now very common among the people of this country, and know what is said *pro* and *con* regarding the questions of the day. There is probably a larger proportion of the members of the national party than of either of the other political parties who are able to " make a good speech," and who are now engaged in writing for the newspapers of the country. They have incessant drill and practice in talking, and the fondness of the masses for oratory gives these propagandists a great opportunity. They are all aggressive and confident, and most of them manifest a degree of exultation in prospect of speedy success. As I have been familiar with their views from the first in the Northwestern States, and for many years past in the three States mentioned before, I have heard little that is new in these recent conversations. Perhaps the chief change is that our friends of the new party now talk a great deal about history, and constantly appeal to its lessons, whereas they formerly derided scornfully the notion of assistance for us from the experience of other nations. A great deal of the history brought forward I confess I never heard of before.

It is true that these thirty-four men are much superior to the majority of the national party, but they, and such.as they, are the true representatives of the masses who have neither opinions nor power of expression, and who are as clay in the hands of the potter under the influence of these workers and organizers. Precisely the same thing is true of the other parties. What these active, capable workingmen think and say is what their silent brethren are acting upon and supporting with their votes.

All these men are very much in earnest, but I could discover no sign of that sense of responsibility which all men of insight feel in undertaking movements which must seriously affect the welfare of many millions of human beings. It seemed to me that they had no adequate conception of the real nature or magnitude of the changes in our national life and society which they were trying to accomplish. Most of them seemed somewhat reckless in regard to possible consequences of these changes. None of them, I think, are acquainted with the later conceptions of history, and its value as a record of the experience of society, of its efforts, illusions, gains, and failures during the ages which have been necessary to develop and establish such civilization and political and social organization as we have attained.

There were differences of opinion among these workingmen upon some points, but it is to be observed that they agree in their belief in "absolute

money," — money that is not a promise to pay,
nor composed of any material having intrinsic
value; in desiring the government to become the
employer of the people by constructing public
works of enormous extent, and in thinking that it
should own and operate railroads, canals, and
telegraphs for the benefit of the people; in favoring government ownership of land, legal prohibition of large accumulations of wealth by individuals, and the substitution, to a great extent, of the
will of the people, as expressed each year (or
each day), for fixed constitutional provisions and
limitations. They agree in thinking lightly of
culture, and in the purpose to legislate and tax
" the money power " out of existence. But none
of them spoke of the need of industry, economy,
or wise self-direction on the part of . their own
class, though they were confident of their ability
to reorganize and direct society. If their undertaking could succeed, we should have wealth without labor, and a system of morals without self-
restraint ; .and instead of the orderly empire of
law we should have " mob-voiced lawlessness,"
anarchy uttered or ordained by the people. I
have seen no reason for thinking we are near the
end of this conflict.

I observed another trait in intellectual character. It appeared to me that very few of these
men had received any education in regard to the
laws, methods, and difficulties of clear and trustworthy thinking. They seemed unconscious of

the danger from illusions, and of the necessity for testing and verifying opinions and theories by patient analysis and comparison. Many of them indeed professed the belief that the direct mental vision or intuition of uneducated men is more valuable, in determining matters connected with legislation and the organization and progress of society, than the trained and disciplined faculties of students or men of culture. They esteem very lightly the judgment or authority of scholars, and believe that American workingmen are entirely competent to understand and decide rightly the problems which have perplexed thoughtful statesmen and patriots for ages. Their faculties have not been trained to analysis or comparison, or to the study, by trustworthy methods, of the relations between causes and effects. They still use very largely the methods of thought of uncivilized or prehistoric men. At every step they are the unconscious prey of illusion, and they are to a great extent incapable of receiving guidance or assistance from anybody wiser than themselves. Their intellectual character is a matter of profound interest to me, because I believe it to be very nearly that of a vast majority of the voters of our country ; and almost precisely that which our existing methods of education are fitted to produce.

THERE are many types or varieties of character
among the workingmen of this country. As acquaintance with many individuals must precede
any useful attempt at classification, I present these
sketches of workingmen I have known without
trying to determine in what degree they are typi-
cal or representative persons. Of course one can
report only what he has seen. Workingmen are
not equally communicative with everybody, and
there are few observers who, to use a phrase common among the workingmen, can " put things together;" few who distinguish what is significant,
or penetrate to the relations between the most familiar facts, or even remember and think about
what they have seen. My acquaintance with
American workingmen in different parts of the
country has impressed me with the essential truth
of the saying that the whole world is everywhere,
and that although many things seem strange or
unusual when first seen, continued observation reveals the existence of similar facts and instances
almost everywhere. Of course the life of workingmen and their families varies in many of its features in different regions. There are observable
diversities of type, in conditions and in character,

as we pass from the mountain mining regions to the farms of the Western prairies or of New England. Manufacturing communities have their peculiarities. Changes in employment modify the character of the population. The establishment of a great factory employing a thousand men or women would produce important social and moral modifications in any community. Wide-spread changes in opinion also affect the prevalent type of character, and in time even the structure of society. The increased hostility to the churches which has been developed in some classes of our population within the last twenty years has already produced in many places a greater feebleness of community. There is not always now, on the part of the people living near each other, so general or vital co-operation for the promotion of the interests of the neighborhood, as formerly existed; and the more definite and active opposition to Christianity in our time has already produced changes in the administration of charity, and, what is more important, in the moral guardianship of the younger and more dependent members of many communities. There is often less interest on the part of society in the establishment of young men in business or profitable industry. Such shifting of currents and tendencies in the life and thought of the age often goes on for some time without being recognized; but no student of the subject believes that great changes can take place in the circumstances, occupations, opinions, habits, and educational conditions of any population without some resulting modification in personal character and the structure of society.

Strong drink is still the greatest evil in the life of multitudes of American workingmen, though the number of those who do not use ardent spirits at all has greatly increased during the last twenty-five years, and is still increasing. Yet there are workingmen everywhere who are fighting this appetite, and trying to throw off the bondage of the habit of indulgence. One such I have known for many years. He was born in New England, and was a member of the first company of soldiers who left Boston for the seat of war at the beginning of the rebellion. He was shot through the hand at Antietam, and receives a pension of five dollars per month from the government. Four or five of his children are in the public schools, and there are two or three smaller ones at home. He has been for several years a shoemaker, working in the large shops or "factories" of a country town. There seems to be nothing loose or defective in his original equipment; he has in almost every respect a fine nature; but he had a hard struggle for several years with the habit of social drinking. It beset him most severely in times of depression, when he was out of work, or after sickness in his family. His pastor once told me of having chanced to see him coming out of a saloon one day while the shops were closed. The clergyman met him with an impetuous expression of grief and disappointment that he should not have cared more for the trials and perplexities of his minister's lot, and should be willing to add thus to his burdens, mentioning several workingmen about whom he had long been anxious, and whom he had tried to encourage and fortify against the appetite for liquor. " If you workingmen go on in this way," he concluded, " how can I have strength or hope to try to do anything ? It is enough to break a man's heart to see that nobody cares about what he is trying so hard to accomplish." The man's face grew white ; he burst into tears, and said, " I did not know you cared so much about it as that. I will never go into such a place again." And the minister thinks he has kept his word.

The life of such a man has its trials and hardships. During many years past he has scarcely ever received more than enough for the subsistence of his family in time of health. He is now able, while working by the piece, to earn a dollar and a half per day. This, with the pension added, amounts at the utmost to about five hundred and thirty dollars per year. Out of this he must pay rent for his house, and provide all that his family can have to live upon. The closest economy consistent with health does not avail to save any considerable part of such an income. But sickness comes to all homes, and most frequently to those of the poor. When it visits a household like this, even if the workman is not kept from the shop by the illness of child or wife, there is unavoidably some increase of expenditure. There can be but very little increase without incurring debts, and in such circumstances how can debts ever be paid ?

Then there are sometimes losses from other causes than sickness in the family. Two or three years ago this man worked for manufacturers who did not (perhaps could not) pay their hands promptly. My friend's children had been ill, and he was straining every nerve to make extra wages, frequently working fifteen hours out of the twenty-four. He had gone on thus for some months, when his employers suddenly closed their shop and left the town. Other creditors seized the stock on hand, and the workmen were left unpaid. The amount due my neighbor was about one hundred and fifty dollars. I went to see him. He was depressed, of course, and indignant, but bore the stroke bravely. It was a serious matter for him. His wife was troubled and anxious lest her husband might, under such discouragement, yield to the temptation he had long withstood, and so lose the mastery of himself he had so hardly won. He was half sick for a day or two, but wise neighbors invited him and his family out for two or three visits. He soon emerged from his depression, and as soon as possible obtained work in another shop. Since then he has not been able to free himself from debt, but he told me recently

6

that with a year of steady work and close economy he can pay all that he owes.

I asked him lately if he was attending the political meetings now being held nightly in the town where he lives. "No," said he; "I do not go at all this year. I joined the greenback people last year, listened to their speeches, and voted their ticket. But their talk has disgusted me. I told my wife they were depending on getting something out of nothing. We are all to be prosperous with very little labor. Now, I don't see how that can be. It may be that poor people are oppressed, and I think myself some things are wrong, and they are hard to bear ; but as I look at it, it takes a deal of hard work to keep this world going on, and it seems to me these labor reformers would only make things worse. One thing I have noticed : I have been out of work sometimes for a few weeks, and even when we had plenty to live on the idleness did me no good." This man is growing in self-control and strength of character. He has a good wife, and his children are doing well in the public schools.

I have observed that workingmen who habitnally drink even the lighter beverages, such as beer and ale, are usually more irritable at home, and are more frequently involved in domestic disturbance and unhappiness, than those who use no liquor. In the towns and cities the children of those who do not drink are commonly more intelligent, quiet, and well behaved than the children

of parents who drink even moderately. This results largely, I suppose, from the fact that men
who do not drink are at home at evening much
more, and their family life becomes more social,
intellectual, and active.

Another hardship and temptation for multitudes of workingmen arises from the fact that
they have been systematically taught by all their
guides that in this country men should "aspire"
to the possession of nearly everything that appears
in any way desirable. The old moral teaching,
which emphasized intelligibly and without mysti-
cism the strength which comes from the repression
of desires, has been to a great extent disused. It
is harder and more painful than formerly for
workingmen and their families to "do without
things." In very few communities has there been
any example of moderation on the part of the
more fortunate classes, and these are not without
some degree of responsibility for the alienation
and discontent recently apparent among workingmen. The unwillingness to begin where they are,
and accept the facts of their situation, with the
wearing, fruitless endeavor to live on a scale requiring an expenditure greater than their income,
is perhaps the chief evil and error in the life of
American workingmen as a class. (Of course
this does not now apply to those who are entirely
without employment.) Would that this evil were
confined to the class of workingmen!

The next story is of a man who is now between forty-five and fifty years of age, who was born in New England. He was from boyhood an earnest abolitionist; was a common soldier and afterward a commissioned officer in the Union army; and has been a farmer and house-carpenter since the close of the war. In speaking of him I feel that I ought to begin with the fullest recognition of the many excellent qualities in his character. He is a man of most amiable and kindly disposition; of great tenderness and benevolence to the poor, the sick, and all who are in distress; a faithful and sympathetic nurse when disease invades the homes of his neighbors; and ready to divide his last crust with those whom others neglect or abuse. He is what people call a well-informed man; his knowledge of what may be learned from the encyclopædias and from good books being above the average attainments even of " cultivated people." Yet he is poorly fitted for life in a world where effects depend upon causes, and most good things have their price in toil. My friend has always been greatly interested in the elevation of mankind, the improvement of society, and the progress of humanity, — to use three phrases which are very dear to him. But he has not been, and is not now, able so to apply and direct his own powers as to gain a subsistence for himself and his family. He once had a farm, which, if it had been managed wisely and cultivated with energy, would have been a sufficient means and source of support, a most comfortable and desirable home. But he would never begin his work at the right time, or follow it persistently after his tardy beginning.

In the late spring, when his neighbors were already plowing their corn, they would sometimes ask each other, " How's the captain's corn ? " And the usual reply would be, " The captain has n't planted yet. Fact is, he has n't got his plans made out for this season's crop." This reply hints at one of my friend's greatest difficulties. His plans are always so large and complex, and all his movements so deliberate, that it is almost impossible for him to begin even the simplest and most ordinary operations of the farm.

He is an inveterate reader, and has read many good books during the long summer days when his labor was sadly needed on his farm. He has always had an especial fondness for the speculative or theoretical side of the physical sciences, and is deeply interested in all labor-saving inventions, and especially in projects which promise great results from apparently trifling causes. He has almost boundless faith in the possibility of such inventions or discoveries. I think he would scarcely be staggered by the announcement that somebody had a plan to warm the polar regions of the globe and cool the tropics, or had found out how to evolve power enough from a pail of water to drive a railway train across the continent. He has a vivid imagination, but it has never been disciplined, or brought into relations with the facts of life.   I think the greatest happiness of his life has been the study of the works of Tyndall, Huxley, and Darwin.   He is very familiar with these, and has eminent delight in Mr. Darwin's speculations regarding the origin and development of animal and human life.   He has good conversational powers, and is a very interesting companion on a journey or in the social circle.

Yet this man, with all these endowments and with good health and ample strength of body and limb, has not been successful in life.   He early began borrowing money for current expenses, for the means of subsistence, mortgaging his farm to secure the payment of these sums, which grew larger and larger, and were never paid.   By and by the whole value of the farm was swallowed up, and he was dispossessed.   He has many children, and the family would often have suffered sharply if it had not been for the patient, laborious industry of the wife and mother, who is not at all poetical or imaginative, who has no great plans or theories, but who has an old-fashioned, practical faith in hard work.   For many years the family has in large measure subsisted upon the scanty proceeds of her work with her sewing-machine.   If she had been seconded by equal industry and application on the part of her husband, they might now have been a prosperous family in a home of their own. Instead of this the man is hopelessly, fatally, in debt.   His credit was gone long ago.

My friend has recently been profoundly inter-

ested in the science of government, and especially
in subjects connected with the financial systems
of different nations. He now attributes the loss
of his farm to fatal mismanagement on the part of
our government, and an evil discrimination in our
national legislation against the workingmen and
in favor of capitalists. His theories of these subjects need not be recorded here at length. They
are essentially the same as those held by most of
the men who think the way can be opened into a
new Garden of Eden for mankind by intrusting
the guidance and control of society to leaders who
have not been spoiled by culture or knowledge.
His expectations have, however, an Oriental rich-
ness of coloring, a breadth and sweep surpassing
all that I have heard or read in the most sanguine
predictions of the prophets of the national party.
The opinions or theories of this class relative to
financial subjects, and other matters connected
with the government and the organization of society, however wild and baseless we may esteem
them, are held naturally by their votaries. Our
fellow-citizens who still display the characteristics
of prehistoric thought are, in an important sense,
logical and consistent. They think as they must
think till they have a different education. These
theories and prepossessions are coherent with their
usual intellectual methods, and with the whole
body of their thought. They are such as should
have been expected, under existing circumstances,
from a class with their equipment and education.

I think the failures of this life can be traced far back, if not entirely to their sources. My friend has always been, as he himself declares, a dreamer and idealist. When he was young he loved to indulge in reverie,—in beautiful and happy imaginings of a world unblighted by evil and suffering. It would probably have required, even in early manhood, strenuous self-restraint, a severe and protracted course of effort and discipline, to overcome this inclination to luxurious, indolent thinking. The habit has so long been firmly fixed that probably no endeavor of which he is now capable would avail to free him from this bondage, a bondage which is in some respects not unlike that of opium or strong drink. His neighbors cannot afford to employ him, because he so often forgets himself or his work. Even in such occupations as require the constant attention and reciprocal activity of two men, such as handling lumber or brick, he becomes oblivious, in the briefest interval, respecting the necessity of coöperation with his fellow-workman.

Our friend has never used intoxicating liquors, having been faithful to his habit of total abstinence even while an officer in the army. An old neighbor and faithful friend of his, who is in no degree blind to his faults, says that the captain would face all possible obloquy in support of an unpopular principle or cause, and that he would undoubtedly meet death unflinchingly at the hands of an angry mob, if that were the penalty for proteeting a helpless woman or child from abuse, or befriending an oppressed negro or Chinaman ; and my own acquaintance with the man leads me to regard this estimate as only just. He is capable of any devotion or sacrifice that would not require faithful, patient industry, and a recognition of the hard facts and conditions of human life in this world. He has always preferred illusions to truth.

At a meeting of a greenback club a few weeks ago, after our friend had made a speech in which representations of the woes of the unemployed millions of American workingmen were mingled with glowing millennial prophecies of the good time coming, " when the people shall have buried the capitalist and the politician in one wide, deep grave," an old farmer gave his neighbors his view of the state of the country : " The man who works for money and then saves it will have it ; but the man who spends good working-days talking politics will never have much of anything. It 's well enough for neighbors to talk over these things on Saturday evenings down at the store, specially if there 's anybody there that knows anything about such matters ; but a good many men about here would rather talk all day on the streets about the hard times and the meanness of the bond-holders than to do an honest day's work. I have been farming here, in the edge of the village, for fifteen years. Before that I farmed in Northern New York. Have always hired one or two hands. Men do not generally work so well of late years as before the war. The high wages just after the war seemed to spoil a good many of them. They acted as if they thought they were working eutirely for their own interest, and not at all for mine. One of my hands told me once — that was in 1865 or 1866 — that while he could make three dollars a day he would n't stand much orderin' around from anybody. I discharged him at once, for I thought he might soon conclude that he owned the farm, instead of me. I always hired men from New York (where I used to live), for six months or a year at a time, till three years ago my wife and I thought that as so many men here were out of employment, and there was real distress on account of it, I ought to give my neighbors a chance to do whatever work I had for hired men. But it has been unprofitable for me, and has not seemed to do them much good. I have not found many men who were ready to go to work at any particular time. Some who had complained bitterly of the hard times, and of not being employed, engaged to work for me, but they never came. Others came so late in the morning and worked so leisurely that it made me tired to see their movements. One man made greenback speeches to me nearly all one day; they were pretty good speeches, too, — of the kind. At night I paid him, and told him I did not feel comfortable in having a man at work in my fields who could speak so well as he. He was very poor and needed every cent he could make,

but I would have paid him pretty good wages to
stay away rather than have him on my place.   I
have tried to have some men work for me who get
help from the town in winter, but I never could
get much out of them."

It is a little more than ten years since a sturdy
young friend of mine, whom the neighbors called
Jim, bought sixty acres of land about two miles
from a thriving country town in one of the largest States.   It was high ground, lying on the first
" bench " or elevation above a river valley or
" bottom," to use terms common in that region.
It had been rendered nearly worthless for agricult-
ure by the use of the upper stratum of clay over
most of its surface, in the manufacture of brick.
Then it had been for a long time part of an un-
settled estate belonging to non-resident heirs, and,
as nobody took care of it, excavations were made
upon it for earth to fill up low-lying lots, and for
road-making, till it was as rough and uninviting a
place as one would see in a day's ride, — made up
mostly of irregular hillocks of clay, small ponds,
and tracts of mire.   At last it was to be sold, and
this young fellow, who had just attained his majority, was the purchaser.   He was an orphan, free
after he was sixteen years of age to make his own
living, and without a dollar in the world, or any
possession but sound health and a strong will.   He
had at that time gone into the army, and after the
war was over he had worked on the farms and in

the stone quarries in the vicinity, and in these five years had saved enough to make a good first payment on this piece of land. He had now to improve his property and finish paying for it. He had a surveyor look over the ground and advise about drains. Then he bought a little scrub mule and an old cart, as he was determined not to go in debt for anything besides the land. He began digging down banks, opening ditches, and filling up ponds. He obtained permission to remove the earth thrown out in enlarging and extending a mill-race not far away, and engaged in carting this on to his land. He planted every foot of his ground that would produce anything, and labored early and late to bring more of it into a state of fitness for cultivation. When obliged to have money, he worked for a few days in the stone quarries. He put up a little cabin on his own ground, and brought an old negro woman from the town to keep house for him.

I sometimes saw him in those days, going 'out to the cabin on Sunday afternoons for a little talk with him. The old woman went to church regularly on Sunday morning, and Jim went along, because, as he said, it kept fellows away whom he did not wish to associate with. I thought this a good reason, and did not press him for others. He did not use tobacco nor any kind of strong drink. "The fact is," he said, "vices are luxuries, and I can't afford to have any." I found that his reputation among the farmers and business men was excellent for industry and faithfulness.   One old man told me that Jim lost less time in getting at his work than any other hand he had ever employed. " He 'll be in the middle of a job, goin' on steady and regular, while other men are sort o' preparin' to get ready."

Last year I visited Jim again. Walking out to his place, I met him driving a span of gigantic mules harnessed to a wagon-load of stone. He stopped his team, and sprang off his load, in order to greet me. Then, as there was a long reach of level road ahead, he invited me to share his seat, and we talked of old times, of the state of the country, and of his affairs. He had made the last payment for his place some months before, owned the team he was driving, and had made various improvements on the land, as he would show me in the afternoon. He told me, among other things, that a few years before he had bought, for a merely nominal sum, the privilege of cleaning the streets of the neighboring town, removing the sweepings to his place for their value as fertilizing material. He said the streets had not been cleaned before, in any thorough or systematic way, and that at first he could not induce even idle men who were in quest of employment to assist in cleaning them for good wages. " No," said one of the colored men, " I'se had pretty hard times ; I'se had to git down pretty low, but I'se never come to that." But Jim soon changed that by going into town on Saturday, when the streets were full of people, and loading up his cart before a crowd of wondering boys. One or two acquaintances jeered good-naturedly ; but Jim soon extended his operations, and hired men and boys to collect the street sweepings, litter from stables and barns, and rubbish from door-yards, all of which enriched his land, and left the town one of the cleanest I have seen, whereas it was formerly a very dirty one. "You see," said he, "my ground will bear a deal of fertilizing. It has a clay subsoil, and will keep all I give it."

In the afternoon we looked over his place together. There was hardly a trace of its old appearance left. All the ground had been brought under cultivation ; a barn had been built, trees planted, and the cabin enlarged. I saw a workbench under a shed, and stopped to look at the tools. "Yes," said Jim, "our workingmen buy too many things ; buy things that they ought to make for themselves. I've saved a good many dollars here, and have n't lost any time, for I should have to go twice to town for each job of repairing done there." In the house the furniture was nearly all home-made. (I have been in scores of the homes of unemployed workingmen, in different parts of our country, during the last five years, where the chairs, tables, and bedsteads were all worn out and breaking down, so that in many instances there was not a safe or comfortable seat in the house. Yet the furniture had all been bought of dealers at high prices, if we consider

its quality and its capacity for use, — or rather
for going to pieces, — and these workingmen were
not able to repair it, or even to make new stools
on which to sit while eating their food. They had
been at work in shops, mills, or factories, and
when these closed had so little power of self-help
that months of idleness passed without anything .
being done to make their homes more comfortable.
In such cases everything that comes into the house,
or that is used about it, must be bought, and requires money for its purchase.)

The old colored woman was still housekeeper.
On shelves against the wall I saw two or three
volumes of Gray's botanies, with some recent
books on chemistry, geology, and mineralogy. "I
thought I would learn something about my own
ground and what grows on it. I have given very
little time to these things, — a few minutes now
and then after dinner, or while the mules were
resting; but it has been a kind of rest to me when
I was tired to look for things, and then try to
learn about them after I had found them. I was
surprised to find so many kinds of plants on this
small piece of ground. I have found several
which the books say are rare, and it is likely
there are many that I have not happened to see."

" Did you have no instruction ? "

" Only from the books, at first, but they are
very plain. All one needs is a start. I was plowing here one day, when a man came along and
asked if he might walk over the field and look at

what grew on my ground. I said, Yes, and asked
if I might go along. So I let my team stand, for
I thought it worth while to leave my work for an
hour if I could learn something. The gentleman
knew about plants, and gave me some good hints,
and said the real good of such studies was in the
discipline or cultivation that we get by observing
and comparing things. It was an hour well spent.
The gentleman advised me to make a list or record of all the plants and trees growing here, and
also of the different minerals and kinds of stone;
but I do not get along very fast with it. Sometimes I wish I could have been here before the
place was worked over so much." There were
many geological and mineralogical specimens in a
little cabinet; a few of them such as would be
highly valued by collectors. " I have come really
to love the place," said my young friend, " but I
am going to leave it soon."

" Why," said I, " why is that ? "

" Well, it is getting to be very comfortable
here, and easy, and I am too young for that.
Whenever I see a rough, wild piece of ground,
that has never had any chance, I feel like taking
hold to see what can be made of it. We never
know what is in such a wild, forsaken place till
we begin to work with it; then the land seems
to take hold and do the best it can. There's a
very rough place out among the hills, a few miles
from here, that I should like to make a partnership with for a few years. It's entirely different

from this, so I shall like it for that. It's full of rocks, and is very uneven, with another kind of soil, and I shall have to learn nearly everything new. I have concluded to buy it."

In the evening Jim harnessed his mules and drove me to town. As we left his gate I said, " You like mules best ? "

He laughed, and answered, " They are not handsome, but in the mud and on rough ground they can do what 's wanted of them, and are worth more than fine horses. I think, sometimes, there 's a good deal of hard mule work wanted in this country. I know when I came here I needed about as much straightening out as this piece of ground; and you remember how it looked. The mules have helped me a little, besides improving the place."

" Have you not wished you had some easier work ? Some of your neighbors here, I believe, think men ought not to work so much or so hard."

" I do not know how it may be with others, — though I think most young fellows are much alike, — but it takes about twelve hours a day to keep me up to what a man ought to be. I am sometimes almost frightened to find how fast the weeds will grow in a fellow's disposition with a little idleness. All sorts of unprofitable and dreamy thoughts come up, and get stronger and stronger. It would not take long to feel meddlesome and envious and sour and discontented. I believe I should soon be a savage if it were not for hard work."

" Do you see much of other young men here?"

" Most of them belong to so many societies in the town that they have no time for anything but their meetings. They wanted me to join all of them, and I asked what they did. So they told me their course of proceeding for the evening. That might do very well for one time, I thought, but they said they did the same things over again every time they came together, and that would not do for me. The young fellows that belong to these societies don't seem to know what to do with themselves when they are at home or alone."

"Do they seem to be well informed?"

" None of us are well informed. A few of us know a little of a good many things, but we know nothing to the bottom. And now this reminds me of what I have for a long time wished to ask you. What shall I read? What can I tell these young men to read? Some of them are not satisfied with the way they are going on. One day I was thinking how reasonable it was that I should know something about the ground I was working over every day, and I wished I could know about the history of this very spot all the way through the old ages, and how it had come to be what it is now. I thought it might help me to know what to do with it. And I should like to know about human society, especially in our own country, — about the changes and steps by which it has come

to be what it is now. I can't find out very well
what it is now, — what is the real condition of
things. I see different people working in different directions. Some of these movements must
be wrong, and I should like to know which I
ought to help and work with. I can't read the
great newspapers. They are too large, and it
would take more time than workingmen can spare
to read them. The writers seem to think people
have nothing else to do but read their long articles. Is there any rather small paper that will
tell the truth and explain things plainly, that I
can read and show to the young men about
here?"

(The same inquiry has been addressed to me
hundreds of times during the last dozen years by
workingmen in nearly all the Northern States,
when I have conversed with them about the state
of the country and the interests and duties of
their class. I have always had to answer that
although we have a few invaluable publications
which are organs of wise and sound thinking, they
are for the most part addressed to the cultivated
classes, and are more elaborate and bookish, as
well as more costly, than reading for workingmen
should be ; and that there is as yet no such means
for the education of the workingmen as such a paper would supply. Of late I have to reflect that,
although I cannot yet point workingmen to such a
newspaper as they need, hundreds of thousands
of them receive each week one that is devoted to

the propagation of theories of government and a philosophy of life which, if generally accepted by its readers, must not only stimulate the growth of erroneous opinions, but also lower the tone and standard of character among American working-men; and this organ of illusion and destructive error, although as large as our leading American newspapers, is supplied to subscribers for twenty-five cents per year. Why should sound and wholesome teaching cost so much more than that which, is mischievous? Although the exponents of prehistoric or uncivilized thought claim to be the friends and representatives of the poor, they are not without means for the propagation of their ideas. They give their publishing enter-prises a vigorous support, and are ready to pay large sums for the services of acceptable speak-ers.) I told my young friend I thought there would be such a paper before many years had passed, and advised him to ask two or three of the most thoughtful young men to join him in taking some of the best newspapers, and to buy such numbers of the magazines as contain articles of special interest and value; and then we parted.

My observation of the life and thought of work-ingmen impresses me with the conviction that the cultivated men of the country are not, in a suffi-cient degree, in communication with the great body of the laboring people; and that a more direct and vital relation between them would be a great gain to both classes. The things which our best and wisest men are saying to each other should be addressed, and in suitable forms of utterance might be addressed, to the workingmen of the nation.

There is danger that we shall accept as necessary and inevitable the permanence of the conditions which have produced our present difficulties; that even our leaders, those who " in their motion are full-welling fountain-heads of change," may not see how imperative is the need of a system of education that shall be so disciplinary of the mass of the people as to make them truly self-governing; or, in other words, to make purely democratic institutions compatible with progress in civilization. Existing means and agencies for the political education of our people are very inadequate. We have depended upon our common schools for results which they alone could not possibly produce.

I suppose few intelligent men now think our chief peril is from communistic outbreaks or revolution. But it is somewhat remarkable that people should so readily conclude that if we are not threatened by this particular danger we have no cause for apprehension; and that the condition and prospects of our country are therefore, on the whole, satisfactory and encouraging. About the utmost mischief in the power of communistic mobs would be the burning of some of our cities, and to accomplish even so much as that they would have to be aided by the accidental concurrence of many favoring conditions. But history shows us that nations have often been lulled into fancied security by their deliverance from one form of danger, while from sources unnoticed or deemed contemptible more serious mischiefs arose, and wrought lasting injury.

Are not the conditions of intellectual soil and atmosphere favorable for the growth of plausible fallacies, of illusions about what can be accomplished by legislation in "lightening the burdens of poverty and toil, and bringing back the days of prosperity to a suffering people," — illusions which will lead the minds of men away from the study of the real problems of the time, and make them more and more impatient and unteachable? May we not reasonably anticipate a long period of wasteful and often very perilous experiments (if we can rightly use the word "experiment" for what is the result of mere impulse and recklessness; for what is undertaken without foresight, carried forward without critical observation or intelligence, and looked back to when it is past with no increase of wisdom from experience), — experiments which will greatly exhaust the national vitality and resources, and which are therefore too costly to be undertaken if they can be avoided? But it is common among cultivated people, who feel, not unreasonably, a kind of awe of the vastness and complexity of our modern life, to urge that each of these mischievous falla-

cies and illusions " will play its part in the education of the people," and that the result of this
educational process is what we must chiefly depend upon for the increase of wisdom among us,
and for the development of such qualities in the
national character as shall secure our continued
progress in civilization.

Let us examine this briefly. We have need of
clear thinking here. A trust in events, in general conditions, and in the influence of the total
environment of society, as the chief means or
sources of change, is one of the prominent features of modern cultivated thought. As it is now
held, this trust, with the scientific and philosophical theories with which it is correlated, marks an
important stage in intellectual and social evolution, but it admits of modification and further development. We are apt to be somewhat dazed
and bewildered by the modern revelations of the
immensity of the universe. Everywhere we en-
counter a tangle and maze of elements, conditions,
and relations, practically of infinite extent; and
in the study of civilization, or the evolution of society, this impression of the slow working of resistless forces, through a limitless complexity of
causes and effects, recurs continually, and with
especial emphasis. If everything around us is the
result of movements which began when the pri-
mordial atoms floated together, where is there
room for us to put in our hand ? What can we
do but wait for events ? The moral or social

world seems to many of the cultivated minds of
our time a great stage for the vast spectaculár
drama of history. It is one of their illusions that
they are only spectators and critics of the play.
But the vast, eternal movement easily incorpo-
rates human and personal effort. A man's thought
or work becomes, in the measure of his wisdom
and personal vitality, a factor in the life of his
time, a source of change, a cause which transmits
some effect to the near future.

But, more specifically, men and nations are commonly educated by events only as the events are
wisely interpreted and explained by competent
teachers and guides. There is no magical power
in the mere succession of occurrences of any kind
to give men wisdom. One insanity or popular delusion may succeed another, leading to any number of disastrous experiments, and the masses may
garner no stores of valuable experience from such
fateful seed-sowing, unless the time brings forward
teachers who can show to the people the meaning,
origin, and tendencies of contemporary events;
who can come to their work with a power of analysis which will enable them to distinguish the
several factors of the life of the time, and a synthetic judgment by which to estimate the national
character, position, and capabilities. The great
need of our people to-day is precisely this wise in-
terpretation of the events of the last twenty years,
this competent explanation of current legislation
and the other important factors of our national

life and thought. Even partisans should be able to appreciate the fact that much of the prevaient dissatisfacton with the older political organizations has been produced by the partisan interpretations of political issues and events so persistently advanced by the newspapers and orators of both parties. The substitution of unreal for real issues has been so general that the people have nearly everywhere recognized it, and many of those whom they formerly trusted are not now believed even when they tell the truth.

WORKINGMEN'S WIVES.

In these studies of American life nothing is invented or purposely colored. They are reports of the experience and talk of persons I have known, and their interest, for me at least, is in the thought of these men and women, in the effect of their circumstances, experience, and total environment upon their intellectual character and activities. In all my acquaintance with the working people, I have observed that the women appear to be depressed and injured less than the men by the hardships of their life. The anxiety and suffering to which so many of them have been exposed during the last few years have usually been borne by the wives of workingmen with superior patience and courage, and they have developed such readiness of resource as yields only to absolute impossibilities. In many cases the wives of workingmen have for several years supported their families almost entirely. While there has been no work for the men, the women have done washing, sewing, and general housework for all who would employ them. Some women do the washing for half a dozen families each week. In such cases their own home-work must be done at night, and on Sunday. But there are few women who have strength for so much work of this kind, and families often live upon what the wife and mother receives for two, three, or four days' work each week. Sometimes the men assist their wives in the home housekeeping, and even in the washing which is taken in for the neighbors, but I have seen few workingmen who seemed able or inclined to render much assistance in women's work, although idle for months together.

Workingmen's wives are, as a class (so far as my acquaintance extends), more saving or economical than their husbands. They have also less dislike for small jobs, and less contempt for the trifling sums received for them. I am compelled to say that many workingmen appear unwilling to accept transient employment, especially if of a kind to which they are not accustomed; but their wives are usually ready for any kind of work, however disagreeable or poorly paid it may be. The men often yield to complete discouragement, and become listless and stupid, and are sour and cross at home, until, unable longer to endure the misery of inaction, they take to the road and become tramps. It is easy to censure the folly of leaving home for work in times like these, but few persons who live comfortably understand the mental strain and torture borne by unemployed workingmen, who see at each meal that every mouthful on the table is really needed by their children. Hunger does not make men philosophical. In the cities and larger towns some work-

ingmen's wives take to drink, as do the men, when
their condition and prospects have become desperate, but among working women who do not drink,
I have never yet seen one relinquish effort and
yield to despair. Even when the wolf has long
been inside the door, and life is a daily struggle
with pinching want, I have noted the silent endurance of workingmen's wives, the effort always
renewed, the spirit which never yields.

One such woman, whom I have known for several years, has often excited my wonder by the
quiet strength and beauty of her character. She
is about thirty-five years of age. Her father was
a prosperous farmer, and she grew up in the large,
old-fashioned farm-house, where the abundance of
hired help made it unnecessary for her to do anything beyond taking care of her own room and
clothing. But she learned housekeeping in the
intervals of attending school, taught school two
or three years near her home, and then married a
business man whose fortune, consisting largely of
landed property, was amply sufficient to promise
a life of comfort, and the opportunities for intellectual improvement which she so much coveted.
Their life was pleasant and prosperous until a few
years after the war. Then her husband sold his
property and removed to a distant State, where he
bought a farm which had been exhausted by bad
tillage, and which required extensive improvements. About this period the approach of the
hard times began to be foreshadowed by a gen-

eral decline in values, to the consequent disappointment of business men who had looked for profits from the continued rise in prices.

Some of the men to whom our friend had sold portions of his property were unable to pay. Loans which he had thought well secured were not repaid, and could not be collected. The man's health declined, and he was obliged to hire all the labor required in the cultivation of his land. It soon appeared to be advisable to sell the farm, as it was rapidly absorbing all that remained of his money, and yielding very little in return. It was sold for an amount much less than the aggregate cost of the land and the improvements. A house was bought in a small town at a price which now seems extravagant. About half of it was paid at the time out of the money received for the farm, and a mortgage on the house given to secure the remainder. Most of these changes now appear to have been unfortunate, but they were such as many business men were making in those years, and to have followed a wiser course would have required a degree of foresight which very few at that time possessed. Our friends soon found themselves without any assured income. The hope of receiving something on various old debts was not relinquished until several years later, but it has never been realized. There were now four persons in the household, the two children being nearly old enough to go to school. The father hoped to find in the village some employ-

ment which would enable him to support his family, but salaries were being rapidly reduced, and
each month added to the number of men seeking
places. About this time the wife was engaged for
some months in sewing straw goods at home for
manufacturers in one of our large cities. It did
not yet appear absolutely necessary for her to earn
money for the sustenance of the family, but she
preferred to help. Their state and prospects became more serious, and the piano was sold. It
had been a marriage gift to the wife from her
mother.

Part of the money obtained by the sale of the
piano was used to buy a sewing-machine ; and
while the husband did what he could as a day laborer, at gardening, farm-work, sawing wood, etc.,
the wife took sewing from a large manufactory of
woolen clothing. The price for her work was
ninety cents per dozen of the garments upon which
she was employed. For several months she used
the sewing-machine fifteen hours per day, and by
working for that length of time she could make
three fourths of a dozen of these garments each
day. She was thus able to earn three and a half
or four dollars per week. But the labor was too
great for her strength, and in less than a year she
was compelled to relinquish it. During this period she was often unable to sleep from the weariness and pain resulting from excessive labor.

The first payment made on the village property
was also the last. All that could be obtained by

the efforts of both husband and wife was often insufficient to supply the family with needed food. The man's strength declined so much that his labor was not very profitable either to himself or to his employers. It became impossible to pay the interest on the debt for the house. now over-due, and the property was surrendered to the for-mer owner. Owing to the great decline in values, it would not now have sold for more than the amount which was still due on it. Since that time this woman has paid rent for the house which she once hoped soon to own. It is but six dollars per month, yet that is a large sum for her. There have been many dark days. After it be-came plain that the work with the sewing-machine could not be kept up, my friend learned to make various small articles of women's apparel then in fashion, and has kept a small store of them at her home for sale, and has taken orders from custom-ers for their manufacture. The family needs for food, as she has told me, three dollars and a half per week, but there have been many times when they lived on a dollar per week. Sometimes in winter they have been without food or fuel. They often live almost wholly upon bread, and have no meat for weeks together. The woman is a mem-ber of a prosperous church, and attends its meet-ings with great regularity.

"Does your minister come to see you?" I in-quired.

"Oh yes."

" Does he know how you are situated ? "

" No."

" Why do you not tell him ? "

" He has not asked me, or spoken of such things, and I would rather converse with him on other subjects."

" But some of your friends in the church are acquainted with your circumstances ? "

" They know that we have nothing to live on but what I earn, except when my husband can do a little work now and then ; but I do not think they know anything about how much or how little we have."   Here she paused, and I saw that she was making an effort to speak quietly.   Her lips moved in silence, but she soon spoke again in the same clear voice : "It is sometimes hard to be told that such and such ladies have remarked that I am always wonderfully well dressed.   It is quite certain that I should have more work if I were ragged and slovenly.   People would interest themselves about me, and give me something to do, if I gave up trying to be neat.   But I can't do that, you know."   And she laughed gayly, though her eyes were ready to overflow.

She possesses in an unusual degree the power, apparently so easy and natural for some women, of dressing with exquisite taste, even with the poorest materials.   My wife says that Mrs. —— would appear well dressed if she had only an Indian blanket, and would somehow make it look about the same as the costume of all women of taste.

People say that she does not look like a working woman. After a few months' rest from work with the sewing-machine she grew stronger, and undertook dress-making, an industry which she still practices. But there are many others engaged in it; many ladies do their own sewing of late, as a measure of necessary economy; and our friend often has great difficulty in obtaining sufficient work. She feels that debt would be failure and ruin. " I could never keep up heart and energy if we were in debt."

" What are your expectations, your hopes, for the next few years? "

" My children have thus far been kept at school; they are doing well in their studies, and I feel that they must, at any cost, have a tolerable education. My daughter, now about fourteen years of age, has a passion for teaching; and it is my utmost ambition, I suppose I may say, to fit her for that work. My hope is that my health and strength may hold out, and that I may have work enough for the support of my family, and especially to pay my house rent."

" Do you ever look back with regret? "

" I have not time, and if I had that would be foolish and useless."

" Do you blame anybody for your hardships? "

" I feel sometimes, as I suppose all women do in such circumstances, like saying, ' If you had only taken my advice, or done as I wished;' but

it would do no good, and I have never allowed
myself to say it."

"Does it seem to you that people are cold and
harsh and unkind?"

"No; they are generally kind-hearted. They
are sometimes thoughtless, but we must expect
that. Not many know much about the lives of
those around them."

"Does your religion help you? is it a real force
and aid?"

"Yes; there are times when I could not go on,
or have the strength I need, without it. I am not
a very pious person, — not enthusiastically religious; I do not expect that God will do my
work for me, or make everything easy and pleasant; but I could not live, I think, without the feeling that his goodness and justice and love are over
all things, and that somehow, in ways I cannot
understand, He is with me and cares for me in the
darkest times. I am obliged to believe that help
is sent me sometimes in answer to prayer."

"Then, why is it not always sent? why is
prayer not always answered?"

"That is not for me to understand."

This woman's religion appears to be a real force
in her life. There seems to be but little mysti-
cism in her thought. She does cheerfully and
courageously all that lies in her power, and en-
dures patiently the hardships she cannot avoid.
She is certainly made stronger by her faith in the
divine goodness, which, in spite of appearances to

the contrary, she believes is at the heart of things, and is a factor in all human affairs. She thinks that human labor, wisdom, and self-sacrifice are necessary for the right direction of human life, individual and social; and that men must learn how to avoid and cure the evils that now afflict society. "God will not do these things for us, but He will help us if we do our best in any good work." She does not seem to have been injured by her harsh and trying experience. I have observed that many women (and men too) are made cynical by hardship; others adopt eccentric theories about religion or the organization of society, and console themselves by a vehement advocacy of those opinions, or steep their faculties in benumbing dreams of the future, losing thus all power and disposition for present struggle. But this woman, while ready for any drudgery that will enable her to support her family, has lost no iota of self-respect, and does not seem to have been in any wise weakened or degraded by trial and suffering. She retains her old interest in culture, especially in literature, and manages to read each year a few good books. She is well acquainted with the writings of the best American and English poets, and likes biography and essays. She converses well, has a fine presence, and is always in request to preside at tables at church fairs and festivals. Our friend's circumstances do not of course permit her to be much in society. She is rarely away from home, and has no traits or qualities that would fit

her to be a reformer of any kind ; but her example and influence are most wholesome and encouraging.

My next story is of a woman who, although a
good housekeeper, has had much to do with the
life in numerous homes besides her own. She is
the wife of a mechanic, an unusually intelligent
and thoughtful man. Their home is in a village
not far from a large city, and there are several
manufacturing towns of considerable importance
in the same region. I became acquainted with
these persons soon after the close of the civil war.
They are so inseparable in their thought and work
that I cannot well write of one alone. The husband had entered the Union army early, and
served to the close of the contest, and they both
felt that their connection with the nation's struggle had been a kind of religious experience to
them. This first drew me to acquaintance with
them. They had a clear idea of a principle of patriotism which should draw men together in times
of peace, and inspire them with a feeling of com-
radeship and of devotion to the interests of their
country. As I was myself at that time thinking
much of these subjects, and becoming more and
more fully convinced of the importance of encouraging and propagating such ideas, I soon became
greatly interested in the thought and activities of
this workingman and his wife. The man had
read much, and was still reading, about govern-

ment and the organization of society, and had a considerable knowledge of history. He talked with his wife about his reading, and often read aloud the most important passages. For some time before I met him he had been troubled by the growing conviction that many things in the best writings on political economy and similar subjects were inapplicable and impracticable in this country, and among the workingmen whom he knew; and it had just occurred to him to inquire whether there are perhaps some special or peculiar conditions or elements in the circumstances and character of society in this country which have not yet been sufficiently considered by our teachers.

At the period referred to, artisans were still making money in the shops and factories of that region, and there was much talk among them about life insurance. We spent many evenings together: my friend reported the discussions which had occurred at the shops during the dinner hour, and read from various books passages bearing upon the subject; his wife told of what the women were saying, and expressed her own judgment in relation to the matters we were considering. While her husband had been in the army she had had much intercourse with the families of workingmen in the village, and since his return they had worked together for the advancement and elevation of the class to which they belonged. They both thought there were serious objections to life insurance, though it might yet be the best thing available, as a method of saving, for many working people.

"Something of the kind is necessary," said the wife, "because the men cannot keep money. As soon as they have a small sum they either wish to buy something with it, or to invest it in a way that will bring them more. Most women can keep money much better than men can. It pleases them to go on adding to the little stock they have hoarded up, and to look at it now and then; but when a man has a few dollars, he is apt to be restless and unhappy till he has expended it."

"But this is a costly way of saving," observed her husband. "I have been at the principal offices in the city. Two of the companies are putting up showy and expensive buildings. Their officers have good salaries, and the commissions allowed to agents are large. Of course all these things are paid for by the people who are insured. The men who are building up and managing this great business of life insurance are doing it for the profit it will bring to them, of course. That is all right, but it will be far more profitable to them than to the working people."

"The women are inclined to like savings-banks better," said his wife; "they think the money would not be so entirely out of their reach."

"They are partly right," the husband replied, "but we are coming to have too many savings-banks and life insurance companies too. The depositors in the savings-banks have no real security for the safety of their money except the honor and foresight of the bank officers. It is always possible in a time like this that the value of real estate securities may decline so much as to fall below the amount for which they are pledged. It is not likely that prices will always keep up."

"I am sure," said the wife, "that men are buying too many things; they make too many improvements; and these things eat up the profits, it seems to me, of all kinds of business about here. If I should buy so much improved machinery for housekeeping, we should soon be in debt instead of saving anything, and that appears to be just what the men are doing. And if so many people go to making shoes and silks and steel rails, it will bring the prices down so that there will be no profit. Besides, I should think we would have more of these things by and by than anybody will want, or can afford to buy. I cannot see that many people, either workingmen or others, are really saving anything except as they insure their lives or deposit something in savings-banks. So I suppose these plans for saving will really benefit people."

"No doubt they will do good in some ways," was the reply, "but much of the money so invested will probably never come back to those who earned it."

" Then there is something very wrong about it," answered the wife, "for the certainty of having what they save is more important for the working people than anything else connected with money. I have thought a great deal about this matter of interest for money as it affects our people. No doubt it is necessary and right for rich men, who loan large sums, and in the great affairs of the business world. But for working people it does harm, and not good. Many of our class are excited and dazzled by the thought of their money increasing, and, as they say, ' piling up while we are asleep,' so that they often risk losing the whole of it by lending it to men who are not to be trusted, or venturing into wild speculations. I suppose some of these things are too deep for me, but I am sure the effect of interest for money is, for many of the working people, very much like the influence of gambling. It gives them unreasonable hopes for the future, and leads them to desire above all things to escape from the necessity of work ; and, as I said, they often lose their money by it."

" Do you not think the ambition to rise above the condition of working people a good feeling, and one to be encouraged ?" I asked.

"No," said she, "I do not. If we are all to rise above the condition of working people, who will be left to do the world's work ? Everybody seems to think it would be very fine, but I can see that such notions are doing mischief. Is it really degrading to work ? It sounds well to talk about our fitting ourselves for something better. There must be some deception in what our teachers are saying about these things. If we could be wise enough and unselfish enough to do our part in every way as working people should, I think we should be more useful in the world, and much happier than we can be by trying to rise to positions which are not suited to us. Five or six of the men at the shops have bought pianos within a year or two. A political speaker from the city spoke of this at the town hall, a few weeks ago, as an evidence of the superiority of American workingmen and their opportunities, and said that laborers in other countries cannot have such things. That is true, I suppose, but I think if our men had been wise they might have found better uses for their money. You can hear one of the instruments now. Our neighbor's daughter is taking lessons. Her teacher tells her it is a great pity she could not have begun sooner, because the work she has done has spoiled her hands for the piano. Her mother does all the hard work now, and her daughter dresses in style and takes care of her hands. It is not at all likely that her playing will ever be the means of real cultivation to herself or of pleasure to others. A year or two ago she was an earnest, industrious girl, affectionate and happy ; now she is affected, discontented, and disagreeable. She wants many things which she cannot possibly have, and has no idea of being serviceable to anybody. Such changes are going on among nearly all the working people that we know, and if there's a great deal of good in them, there's some harm too."

" Well, wife," said her husband, " tell us, since you are in the way of it, what you think the working people ought to aim at, and what they most need."

" We ought to do our work well and faithfully, so as to be really of service to our employers and to the country. We need to feel more interest in one another as a class, without any enmity toward other people, and to help and encourage one another to gain more of such kinds of knowledge as will be of use to us in our circumstances and way of living. The knowledge that makes the working people dissatisfied with their lot is no blessing, and it is not a kindness to give it to them. We need somebody to tell us and teach us what would be most useful to us. But I can see that the women need to know how to cook a great deal better than they do now, and how to keep their houses and things about them in a wholesome condition, so as not to invite disease into their families. They need to feel more responsibility for their children every way. And then — I must come back to that — the working people need some way of saving money that will be absolutely safe, so that they can be perfectly certain of having it when they want it. Whenever men have steady work, even at moderate wages, they can save something, and they ought to lay by a little at a time, till each family has two, three, or four hundred dollars, as a provision against sickness or possible lack of employment; or has a little

sum for each of the children as they grow up and
begin life for themselves, and perhaps some small
provision for the old age of the parents. To use
all our earnings as we go along has an unfavorable
and demoralizing effect. To bind ourselves by a
resolution to save a small part of each week's income is a useful discipline, — one that we all require. It teaches us to be able to do without
some things that we could have, and that is a kind
of education that would be good for everybody.
But the uncertainty about receiving their money
does more than anything else to discourage the
working people from trying to save. I have
thought a great deal about this, and it seems to
me a very important matter, and one that the wise
men of the nation might well think about. I do
not know anything about the science of government, but there must be something very imperfect in our civilization, or the organization of society, when all the wisdom of this great country
and all the power of the government cannot give
a laboring man who saves fifty dollars any security that he shall have it returned to him when he
needs it. I have sometimes seen such mischief
and suffering result from this state of things that
I could not sleep, and I have spent many hours in
trying to think out some plan for changing it.
Whenever money that is loaned or put in a savings-bank is lost, it makes workingmen reckless
and improvident."

" Tell our friend about your plan," said her

husband, "and perhaps he will say what he thinks of it."

"My plan seems to me a very simple one. It is for the national government to receive money from the people at the post-offices everywhere, and give them certificates of deposit, charging a small fee to pay for the clerical labor involved. The important thing, as I look at it, is that the government is not to pay interest on these deposits. Even if only two or three per cent., or only one per cent., were proposed, there would be serious objections to such a system ; but I cannot see how this plan could do any harm, or why there should be any great difficulty in putting it into practical operation."

"The present organization and character of life insurance and savings-bank business," remarked the husband, "tends to produce everywhere an increasing feebleness of community; and anything that does that works an injury for which nothing can be sufficient compensation. Every life insurance company and savings-bank is a partnership made up of the men who establish the business and of all who invest money in it, — that is, the depositors and those who are insured. The thousands of men whose earnings furnish so large a proportion of the capital have no voice or power in the management or direction of the business. But what is much worse than this, the partners are not acquainted with each other. The managers do not live in the same community with their

partners in the business, and they possess none of
those common interests and responsibilities which
proximity naturally tends to establish. In anything so important in its effects upon character
and the chief interests of society, each community,
village, or neighborhood should, as it seems to me,
organize and direct its own business. If I lend
money to my neighbor, he is more apt to conduct
his business carefully, and to repay me honestly,
because he is my neighbor. When the working
people have put their money into the hands of
men in the city whom they have never seen, they
may feel more interest in the welfare of the city
people ; yet this is a barren kind of interest, as
there can be no personal relations between them ;
but the working people will feel less interest in
their own town and in the welfare of their fellow-citizens and neighbors here. I think our
money, our business, our interests, should, as far
as possible, all be here, where we live, and that
we should all be concerned and responsible for the
welfare of all the members of the community. If
we have savings-banks or life insurance, the entire
business should be here, all the officers our own
citizens, and no money should be drawn from the
people of other places. There should be no expensive buildings, and as little as possible of the
element of speculation in the business, but the
greatest possible degree of certainty in the pres-
ervation of the funds. But the life insurance
which I think most important is that which con-

sists in the strength of community among the people of each village or small town ; in their neighborly good-will, interest, and practical kindness for each other ; in their coöperation in what we may call the moral control and administration of the community ; in the education, protection, and guidance of all its members ; in the repression of license, of ignorance, idleness, and all other vices which seriously threaten social or public interest."

I have not room for any further report of these conversations. My friends still live in the same village. Visiting them early last summer, I found that most of these opinions had been confirmed by observation and experience of the effect of trial and hardship upon the working people. This man always advised his neighbors against trades-unions and secret societies of every kind, but urged them to have places of meeting where anybody might come and talk. Such open clubs have from time to time been sustained by the workingmen there, and have been useful. When the general prostration of business and industry reached the place, my friend had saved nearly a thousand dollars, but had not insured his life, or put his money into a bank. He had loaned it without interest in sums of one or two hundred dollars to business men who were his neighbors. It was all repaid him ; but he told me that a man who had about two hundred dollars of his money came to his house one evening, and said, " Here is your money. I cannot go on much longer, and there

will not be much for anybody, I fear. This is a
personal matter, and I cannot have you lose anything." At one time all the laborers in the shops
and mills were discharged, and a few months' idleness reduced some of them to great straits. My
friend then began lending small sums, without interest, to the most needy workmen, — from two
to twenty-five dollars to each. He says most of
the money has been repaid, and loaned again so
often that the aggregate is more than four thousand dollars. He has lost about one third of his
money, as he supposes, finally. Some of the men
who had it have gone away, and he has lost sight
of them, and a few have died. "But," he says,
"the good and help of it all were so great that I
do not regret a dollar of it." He still thinks this
the best kind of life insurance. His wife has
taught the women how to make old clothing over
again to the best advantage, how to cook beef-
bones so as to obtain much food from what they
had before thrown away (by long boiling to extract all the nutritious elements), to utilize scraps
and remnants of all kinds, and to avoid dangers
to health from foul cellars and bad drainage. The
two have influenced in a notable degree the life
of the village. This report of our conversations is
from notes made at the time many years ago. I
then preserved these records of the talk of a
workingman and his wife, because I thought they
contained some germs, at least, of genuine American thought. The man was born in Vermont, and

the woman in Massachusetts. The families of both have been in this country more than a hundred and fifty years, and have always been working people, and, as my friends say, " none of them were ever 'in better circumstances;' they all had to work for their living, so their descendants have not had to 'come down in the world.'"

I have for many years enjoyed acquaintance with a woman whose home overlooks the great prairies of Southeastern Kansas. Twenty-five or thirty years ago, as she has told me, it was common, where she grew up, for girls engaged to be married to go out to service and earn money for the purchase of their housekeeping outfit. She was in her sixteenth year when she left home for this purpose. Her girlhood had been happy and busy. Her parents lived on a small farm. There were many daughters, and they learned to love the freedom of out-door work in haying and corn-planting time. Idleness and piano-playing and the modern styles of dress had not then become fashionable among young women in that region. An earnest, practical spirit ruled the somewhat primitive society, and the better class of young people had a real thirst for knowledge and improvement. The few books and newspapers were passed from hand to hand, and read in almost every house of the neighborhood. My friend says there is much more reading among the young people now, but the books read are not, where she is acquainted, equal in character to those with which she was familiar in her girlhood. They are less thoughtful, and require less mental exertion on the part of the reader.

She was married at seventeen, and soon afterwards set out on the westward journey of a thousand miles to the region in which she was to find, or rather make, her home. The young couple had money to purchase enough wild prairie land for a farm, and to supply the means of living till they could raise the first crop of corn, but not much more. The grassy plains stretching away to the horizon on every side showed few human habitations. There were at first about a dozen houses within as many miles, and within that distance all were neighbors. But there were new arrivals every year, and life soon became less lonely, or at least less solitary, for the young wife, who battled bravely against home-sickness, and threw herself with energy into all the activities of her new sphere of action. The settlers in the neighborhood represented nearly all parts of the country, except the Pacific coast. There were families from New England and the Middle and Southern Atlantic States, and from the different regions of the great Mississippi Valley, north and south. One of the first things in the new life which impressed this young woman was the fact that the moral differences between the life around her and that to which she had been accustomed all seemed to have been produced by a lowering of the old standards. Men

9

who used profane language acknowledged that
they had not done so in their old homes; some
who had brought letters of fellowship from Eastern churches went hunting on Sundays. Nearly
everybody made and received visits on that day,
and it was a jolly, social holiday. The new citizens and neighbors were good men and women;
there were few coarse or vicious persons among
them, but there was a strong and general tendency
to revert to a much lower type of civilization than
any of them had been acquainted with in the older
portions of the country. This facility in adopting
lower standards, so manifest all about her, caused
the young woman many an hour of anxious, painful thought. It was by no means easy to determine what would be right or wise for herself under the new conditions of her life. Here was a
modest, quiet girl, with no one to advise her, with
no one at first even to understand her, who saw
that society was in process of formation around
her, and felt that some very important elements
and influences were wanting, the lack of which
she was sure would be felt more and more as an
evil and injury as inclination hardened into habit,
and tendencies became fixed in custom. Her interest was the greater because her husband appeared not at all disposed to resist the influences
which excited her distrust. He grew fond of rang-
ing over the prairies with his gun, and steady
work on the farm seemed to affect his health un-
favorably. When several men worked together he

was willing to share in the labor for the sake of companionship, but solitary employment grew more and more distasteful to him. This often led to exchanges of work and other plans for enjoying the society of some of his neighbors, who, like himself, liked conversation so much that work seemed an interruption and an impertinence. His farm and dwelling soon showed signs of neglect and inefficiency, and it was not long till he had contracted debts which the surplus productions of the farm were not sufficient to pay.

After long and painful resistance to a conviction which seemed a kind of disloyalty to her husband, the young wife was compelled to recognize the fact that the wisdom, energy, and responsibility properly belonging to the head of a family were required of her, and that unless her resources proved equal to the unexpected demand, her home life was likely to prove a failure, a life-long disappointment and misery. There was a period of wild and lonely bitterness, and then she quietly accepted her lot, and resolutely entered upon her work of building the temple of home upon better foundations, and of trying to cultivate and encourage as much as possible all the higher elements and aptitudes of her husband's character. She wished, as I suppose most women do, to look up to her husband; to feel that he was her head; to respect his superior strength and authority. But she set forward to make the best of everything, and soon developed a kind of happiness in cour-

ageous effort and endurance. She had much to
endure. More than once the homestead itself has
been imperiled by bad management. But the
business men of the region gradually recognized
the fact that when debts were paid it was by the
wife's economy and energy, and the danger from
the husband's injudicious investments and engage-
ments lessened as the years passed. While she
was thus endeavoring to do her part faithfully at
home, her interest in the life around her grew
more profound and serious. She told her husband
of her feelings and desires regarding the intellectual and moral condition and needs of their neighborhood, and asked his counsel as to her own
course. He thought that any effort to influence
their neighbors would probably be resented by
them as an officious and unfriendly interference,
and, while deploring the want of moral and religious teaching in the region about them, was of
the opinion that people should be left to the teaching of experience. "If they do wrong and get into
trouble, they will learn to do better next time."
Still he did not more decidedly oppose her wishes,
and she felt that the way was clear for her doing
what she could. But what should she attempt?
Although herself earnestly religious, she thought
it not wise to undertake teaching religion directly
or specifically. What she did may appear rather
shocking to many good people, but I can only report the truth. The time was approaching for a
great Sunday visit at her house. It was her turn

to entertain her neighbors. Some fifteen or twenty persons, old and young, would dine with her, and spend the afternoon in conversation and such amusements as they were accustomed to enjoy or might improvise for the occasion. The aimless and thoughtless character of the talk in these social meetings had given my friend much discomfort. It had no direction or purpose, but depended upon mere impulse and accident in its selection of subjects. Its tone was often rather low, and there was never, as she said, anything profitable. If, as often happened, a young person made a serious or thoughtful remark, some older member of the circle would make it the point of a joke or repartee. This young woman's beginning, that Sunday afternoon, for the regeneration of society, was a series of *tableaux vivants*, based on the pictures in a copy of Shakespeare's plays. Everybody was delighted, and there was an unexpected and most gratifying desire to know what it was all about, — who the soldiers and ladies were who had been represented, and what they had done. " Tell us about them," said the young people. Her strength was failing. The battle had been fought, and she had gained the victory. She could not tell stories now. Years afterward she told me of her gratitude to a gentleman present, a physician who, profoundly touched by the change which he felt had passed upon their association, said earnestly, " Not now; we have had enough for to-day. I have the books, — Shakespeare and the English histories, that tell about it all. If any of you will .stop at my house, my wife will show them to you. It is time for us to go now." And with a respectful dignity of manner which awed his neighbors he advanced to the centre of the room and took leave of his hostess. Everybody followed his example.

The next day the doctor rode a few miles out of his course across the prairie, to call on this new acquaintance. They had a long conversation, and she told him of her feelings regarding the community, — of her fervent wish for the beginning of a better order of things. " Well," said the doctor, " we have had the beginning. We will meet at my .house next time. Come over, you and your husband, on Saturday afternoon, and we will make our plans for the entertainment." He was always afterward her faithful ally. It proved, as he said, that a beginning had been made.

The Sunday visits grew into meetings for read, ing, music, and conversation. From the first the mirth was less boisterous and the talk more thoughtful, but there was no loss of real freedom or geniality. I have always wondered most that my friend did not try to do too much. But the hour had come, and the woman. And she could not only do what the occasion required of her; what was quite as necessary to her success, she knew how to choose her marshals. People seemed to develop new capabilities under her influence. Her home life was always trying in many ways.

It was necessary to hire some labor to assist in bringing the land into cultivation, and in order to have means for this she took two or three boarders, men from the East working upon new farms in the vicinity, who had not brought their families with them. The people for many miles around came to depend upon her superior judgment and readiness of resource as a nurse in all cases of severe illness of women and children. Her kindly arms were the first resting-place for scores of little ones upon their arrival in this strange, new world, and she closed the weary eyes of age as the shadows deepened of " the night before the eternal morning." Young lovers came to her, sure of one friend who would not smile at their perplexities and disappointments, nor break the kindly silence which guarded the secret of their pains or joys. No bride's attire could be designed without her judgment. Few social enterprises were regarded as well begun without the sanction of some suggestion from her.

She had no children of her own, but two or three years after marriage she adopted two motherless little boys. One was two years old, but the other had come into life as his mother passed out of it. Never had orphaned babes a tenderer foster-mother. As they grew older, others like them were brought, one after another, to this house of refuge. Some remained for a short time, until they set their little faces toward the land where their mothers had gone before them. Others

were nourished and guided until suitable homes
could be found for them elsewhere.   When a little child was left motherless by the death of a
betrayed and forsaken woman, the neighbors said,
" Mrs. —— will take it," and under her guidance
the child whose life was a legacy of shame has
grown to be a young man of unusual promise.

She has done nearly all the work of her housekeeping, including for many years past a considerable dairy, with sometimes a little assistance for a
few weeks when she is threatened with complete
exhaustion of her strength.   Her health has suffered greatly from her long-continued over-exer-
tion.   But her culture has gone forward, fed not
only by her rich and varied experience of life, but
also from the best literature of our time.   She has
read much ; I can scarcely say how it has been
possible for her to do so, but when I was for a
short time at her house, four years ago, I observed
that an open book lay always within her reach,
and that it was often glanced at for a minute or
two in some pause of the culinary processes, or a
passage would be read now and then in connection
with the conversation.   She writes well, in easy,
graphic narrative, with a clear and vital expression of thought and sentiment.   A few articles
from her pen have been published in Eastern
newspapers, and she has written much for the
papers of her own county.   Her experience would
be a treasure to a writer of fiction.   At the time
referred to I was looking into the geology and

botany of the State in which she lives, driving across the country, in fine weather, in an open carriage. On two or three occasions I asked her to accompany me. Her enjoyment of the open air, of the dewy brightness of the morning, of the sultry summer noon brooding over the wide lands, was as fresh as that of a child. But what interested me most was her reception by the people. As we drove along the roads, and sometimes crossed the great farms where she knew the way, the men everywhere dropped their work, or left their teams standing, and hastened across the fields to greet her. They begged us to stop at their homes to see their wives; and where the house was near the women were called out. I noted a repressed intensity of feeling on their part, like that of lovers meeting in the presence of strangers. She seemed to be in complete sympathy with every one, and received their affectionate homage with quiet, frank delight. Afterward, when I met the physician, her early friend, and still her co-worker in various schemes for popular culture and improvement, he told me the story of her work. (Every one I saw had something to tell of her kindness or wisdom.) He thought it one of the most noticeable features of her life and influence that she inspired all the men with profound respect and admiration, and yet no woman ever felt in the slightest degree jealous of her. I dined with the doctor, and his wife told me the same thing. Said she, "We women all love her, and the men adore her."

The country is much changed since she made it her home. The great valley is populous now. There are half a dozen churches of different denominations within easy reach of her dwelling. She has not joined any of them, but often attends the meetings at two or three of the nearest. The ministers all visit her, and all regard her as a valuable friend and assistant in their work. No one appears to have thought her capable of sectarian feeling. One feature of the work of the Sunday reading club has been the establishment of a neighborhood library. The plan of dining together on Sundays was given up after the first year, as involving too great labor for the hostess, and also because it was felt that the convivial element and interest should be subordinated to the higher objects of the meetings. Most of the people now go to church in the morning, and a few meet still in the afternoon for reading and conversation. A recent letter says, " When the Eastern war came on we obtained a few books and maps (very cheap little things they were), and thought we would give a week or two to learning about it. But our studies grew like the war itself, and we were led to the history of the Turks and of Greece, and kept on for many months. We should never have known Curtius's and Finlay's wonderful histories if it had not been for this war. We even got into the history of the Holy Roman Empire. I forget how it came in, but we read Bryce's little book." They gave a good deal of time to Biblical studies a few years ago, and did not quarrel. My friend says that one of the most stubborn evils with which they have had to contend is the deluge of worthless reading matter which has within a few years extended to that region. She thinks it would be better for people not to read at all than that they should be miseducated by the writings of persons without culture or knowledge.

As we rode homeward on the last day of my visit, I asked her what was still most needed by the people of the valley. She said, " They need discipline, the power and habit of self-restraint and self-direction in nearly everything, but especially in their use of money. They are full of life, and love good living, — love to ' have things.' They might all be rich, but they are so impulsive and extravagant that most of them are in debt, and are often pressed and harassed by their inability to pay their notes when they are due. It is absurd that this should be so in a country with such resources as this region possesses. If we only had some good, convenient way of taking the women's money, whenever they have saved a few dollars, and keeping it for them, they would soon grow more economical. As it is, they always say, ' It is my money, and if I do not buy something with it my husband will spend it for something that will do me no good.' They have little foresight of possible future needs ; but the worst difficulty is that they cannot keep money, and have no place to put it where it will be safe. Some of the girls who are at work about here leave their money with me, but I wish there were some officer, somebody appointed by the government, to take care of people's money, and keep it safely for them. Could it not be so?"

"What have been your greatest difficulties and discouragements?"

"My own lack of ability for the work of life, the want of opportunity for acquiring the culture I need, and the general disposition of.people to be contented with low things."

Both the parents of this woman are descendants of families who removed from Virginia to Ohio about the first of this century ; their ancestors were from England, and ·came to Virginia in very early times.

THE CAREER OF A CAPITALIST.

THIS story is not a warning. It outlines the life of a man belonging to a class against whom there has been much clamor in this country during the last few years. He is a capitalist. According to the teaching of the reformers he is a non-producer, a man who lives by the labor of others, and therefore an oppressor of those whose toil has given him his wealth. It is indeed true that he has never worked with his own hands since the time when, in his early boyhood, he engaged in catching fish for the markets of his native town. Pursuing this industry for a few weeks, he found himself possessed of an accumulation of small silver coins amounting to about twenty-five dollars. The money was for some reason put aside, and is still preserved by his children. " This," he once said to me, " is the first and last money that I ever earned by my own manual labor." His home is on one of the great peninsulas of our Atlantic coast, at the head of navigation on a small river, which permits the passage of vessels of a thousand tons burden. He is fifty-six years old, and still lives on the spot where he was born. His early education was inconsiderable in extent, and so unsystematic that it did not even give him an idea of the methods by which knowledge might be acquired. When he was married he could read but very imperfectly ; but his young wife insisted upon his taking a daily newspaper, and then with affectionate firmness required him to read it through each evening. At first there was much that he did not understand, but he learned the art of wise and stimulating inquiry, and so drew from those about him whatever knowledge they possessed. This habit still gives his conversation a remarkable interest and vitality. He appears to have been able to carry unanswered questions in his mind for any length of time, until some new source of information was revealed.

He was left an orphan when about seventeen years of age, and the next year entered upon the life of a man of business. His father had been the proprietor of a country store with a trade of about forty thousand dollars a year. After his death two of his brothers, who settled the affairs of his estate, decided to continue the business, admitting their nephew, our young friend, to a partnership with them. He received from the estate of his father about fifteen hundred dollars. The affairs of a country store at that time embraced the sale of everything the people of the region needed for use, and the purchase of everything they wished to sell. There was not yet any separation of the different lines or departments of trade, such as dry goods, groceries, hardware, clothing, millinery, etc., but articles belonging to all these classes, and

many others, were sold at the same place, which
also afforded a market for whatever was produced
or manufactured in the surrounding country. The
store was the great vital centre for the life of the
region, for the reception and distribution of everything. There the farmers bought their plows,
harness, shovels, hoes and scythes, hats and shoes
(most of their clothing was manufactured at home
in those days), and there they sold their wheat and
corn, bacon, hay, and other productions of their
farms. Thither their wives and daughters carried young fowls, eggs and butter, and home-made
cloth, and took away in return calicoes, muslin de
laines, bonnets, ribbons, combs, and needles. Here
the wood-cutters bought their axes; the handles
were generally made by somebody possessing un-
common dexterity in this particular manufacture,
and brought to the store for sale. (There are
very few men who can make a good axe-handle;
not so many, probably, as write poetry for the
magazines.) The plans for new undertakings and
enterprises were generally discussed and arranged
at the store, and it had important relations to the
social life of the people. There were opportunities for a genuine and useful education in such a
place, and our young friend entered with hearty
interest upon his new course of life.

He soon came to have a large share in the
organization, direction, and management of the
business, and in a few years became its real head.
He was always a close observer of men, and of the

effect upon them of their circumstances and occu-
patiou. He early became convinced that the interests of a community or country are advanced
by increasing the number of employers, — of men
who direct and pay for the labor of others. He
observed that many men lack capacity for the wise
direction and organization of their own labor,
while they are highly useful and successful when
working for a competent employer. Others possess qualities of mind and character which fit them
to be leaders or masters of the industry of others.
When our friend saw these qualities in the men
around him, he felt a strong desire that they
should have means and opportunities for their development and practical application in some suitable sphere of action. As his business increased
and brought him facilities for extending it in new
directions, he began to confer with some of the
young men of the neighborhood in regard to their
employment and wages. Most of them worked
by the day, at cutting and hauling wood, burning
charcoal, and similar occupations, but there was
not yet in the region any systematic industry
which afforded regular or profitable occupation to
the people. Men were often idle for weeks together. The country needed men to employ and
lead the labor of their neighbors.

So our friend said one day to a young married
man who lived near him, " You are making shoes,
I believe ? "

" Yes, when anybody wants them, and I can
get money to buy stock."

" Why don't you open a shop, and hire two or three hands ? There is young so-and-so, who is doing nothing. He can whittle out anything with a jack-knife, and he ought to have something to whittle that will be of use. He would soon learn ; and you could find one or two more."

" Why, do you think I could get work enough?"

" Well, there are a good many people about here that wear shoes. How much are you making now ? "

" Oh, perhaps a dollar and a half a day, when I have work."

" Well, there is that little house of mine on the corner. You can have that free of rent, and I will let you have money to buy stock. I will insure you your dollar and a half a day ; you shall pay me interest at the legal rate for the money you have from me, and we will divide the profits equally."

The shoe shop was opened, and was successful. It was enlarged in a year or two, and for many years gave steady and profitable employment to a considerable number of men.

By arrangements essentially similar our friend formed partnerships, during the first twenty-five years of his business life, with harness-makers, blacksmiths, wheelwrights, tinsmiths, lumbermen, lime-burners, oystermen, farmers, and manufacturers. He has had scores of such partnerships with wood-cutters and charcoal burners. In the same way he has supplied means for building and operating numerous flouring and saw mills, using both steam and water power. He has owned farms and timber lands in South Carolina, Virginia, Maryland, New Jersey, Pennsylvania, New York, and Ohio, with stores in each region to supply his farmers and the laborers at his mills. Thousands of men have been employed in connection with these enterprises, and hundreds of them enabled to become in their turn employers and organizers of labor. In many instances men have worked for our friend, and with him, during a term longer than that of an average life-time. Almost always the relations of employer and laborer, and of business partnership, have passed into those of personal friendship; and when, as has often occurred, men have wished to leave him to go into business for themselves, he has felt a genuine interest in their undertakings, and done what he could to promote their success. Those who have worked for him longest say that he never employs a man merely for what he can get out of him.

Many years ago he took a young carpenter into partnership, and engaged in ship-building. The oyster fisheries along the coast near him are of great excellence, and furnish employment for thousands of men with their vessels. Of many of these boats, constructed in his ship-yard, our friend retains a share in the ownership, and this relation with the fishermen has promoted steadiness, industry, and sobriety among them in a marked degree. The larger vessels, of from eight hundred to a thousand tons burden, built under his supervision, are known in every sea for the superiority of all the materials used in their construction, and the careful honesty of the work. Many of these he owns in part.

The first carts that were ever taken across the mountains from Acapulco to Oaxaca were made in our friend's shops, and sent out to an acquaintance who had a building contract in the latter city. They were objects of great interest to the native workmen, who were eager to be permitted to use them in transporting the stone and other building materials which they had been carrying. A dozen mules were harnessed, and with some difficulty fastened to the " new carriages." When the first cart, drawn by a rather diminutive mule, was brought to the place where it was to be loaded, the laborers swarmed around it, and piled so much stone into the rear of the vehicle that it tipped over backward and lifted the astonished mule into the air, where it hung and struggled until the removal of the stone restored it to its normal position on the ground.

Some fifteen years ago our friend became desirous of finding some means for preserving and utilizing the enormous quantities of fruit produced in the region in which he lives. He erected a large building and put in the necessary machinery for canning fruit, and this has ever since, during the season for the business, afforded employment to about one hundred women and more than half as many men. The principal products canned are peaches and tomatoes, and of these many millions of pounds have been used, and the goods are known in all the markets of the world. This is an industry which produces and stimulates many others.

The little straggling hamlet in which the young man began his business life has become a handsome and important town, with seven or eight thousand inhabitants, most of them operatives employed in manufacturing industries, — in the production of glass, iron, cotton and woolen goods, shoes, buttons, chemicals, etc. There is probably not one of these industries which was not in some way aided by our friend in the earlier stages of its growth. For many years there were but few men engaged in business of any kind in the town who had not been employed by him, or associated with him in such relations as I have described. The original character of the site of the town made the construction of suitable streets a matter of some difficulty and of a great deal of labor, and to this object our friend has devoted much time and effort. For such work he has never accepted any compensation, regarding all measures for the improvement of the place as matters of enlightened self-interest for business men rather than of duty.

The circumstances of most of the population, their employments and general environment, have been such as favored the development of habits of intemperance. Some of the largest manufactories are closed for two months in summer, and during this time the men and boys are idle. They have good wages during the remainder of the year, and it is not wonderful that drinking and gambling should seem to them only natural amusements and diversions during this long holiday. These industrial and social conditions have given the friends of order, sobriety, and good morals cause for much anxiety, and for constant effort in endeavoring to counteract these unfavorable tendencies. The influence of the various churches of the place, Methodist, Presbyterian, and Roman Catholic, has been highly effective among the operatives as a means of moral restraint and guidance. The public schools of the town have more than average excellence, and the place has one of the best Kindergartens in the country. (It is a real Kindergarten, and not a travesty of Fröbel's principles.) There is a valuable public library with several reading-rooms. Temperance societies of various kinds have rendered important assistance in the mental and moral education of the workingmen. For several years past there has been but little intoxicating liquor sold in the place. All these agencies for the promotion of the most important ends for which society exists have received assistance, encouragement, and sympathy from our friend, and people know beforehand that he may be counted amongst the supporters of any measure likely to advance the interests of the community.

He is the most quiet and unobtrusive of men; he never makes speeches or addresses public meetings, and in arranging matters of business never rambles away from the subject in hand to irrelevant topics. I think he does not belong to any church, but he understands the value of the church in the community, and has a genuine fraternal esteem for all who are laboring to overcome evil and promote good-will among men. He is eminently conscientious, gentle, and forbearing, simply and silently religious. In society his manner is marked by a quiet cordial dignity. He is eminently social, and little children, strangers, and diffident people are at ease with him at once. He likes to entertain his friends by giving them the freedom of his house, the use of horses and carriages, and other means of diversion, while he joins them from time to time with apparently equal interest in whatever his guests prefer as the pursuit of the hour. If a new game is introduced for the children, or young people, he learns it with them, and engages in it with a zest as great as theirs. I think no visitor at his house ever left it without wishing to return.

He has a cultivated and interesting family. His own experience of the disadvantages resulting from the want of culture in early life has led him to give his children an unusually judicious and practical education. His principal recreation consists in hearing his wife or daughters read, commonly some of the works of American authors of our own time. (His old friend, the daily newspaper with which he began his education, is still faithfully read, as it has been for all the years from the first.) He enjoys the writings of our principal American poets, likes biography and travels, and has an especial fondness for books that describe clearly the character, resources, and productions of different countries, with the habits and industries of the people, and the particular conditions under which society exists in various parts of the world. His house is frequented by intelligent and cultivated men and women from different parts of the country, and is one of the chief intellectual and social centres of the region where he lives. A score or so of his neighbors have for some years assembled there once a fortnight for the purpose of reading Shakespeare's plays. No one participates with heartier interest than our friend in the work of this little club. He always wishes to know the meaning of what is read, and is not satisfied till he has learned whatever is attainable about the historical personages or occurrences mentioned in the play.

He likes to see the best actors occasionally. He unites, in as great degree as any man I have ever known, the wondering, receptive spirit of a child with the critical analysis and judgment of a mature and cultivated intellect. He has a genuine enjoyment of good pictures, and prefers small,

quiet landscapes. He is always greatly interested
in machinery, and readily understands its construction and movements. I have met few persons
who saw and comprehended so much as he of the
exhibition in Philadelphia in 1876. He has great
delight in the miscroscope and its revelations. He
is very fond of flowers, and has always been a
close observer of the forms and habits of plants.
When some friends were setting out from his
house, a few years ago, upon a botanical excursion,
he joined them, and on hearing various flowers
and plants described was able to tell where they
grew twenty-five or thirty years before, though
he did not know their names.

He appears to have no eccentricities. He never
uses profane language or ardent spirits. When he
was young, rum was sold at every country store,
but his father had refused to keep it for several
years before his death, and our friend never sold a
drop of intoxicating liquor of any kind. He was
an earnest anti-slavery man, and ever since the
end of the war he has been deeply interested in
the development and prosperity of the Southern
States of the Union. He is cordially patriotic,
and feels much interest in politics, but is not a
partisan, and seems able to recognize true worth
and excellence in all parties and classes. He has
always been solicitous for the diffusion of sound
and practical ideas among the laboring people,
having comprehended at an early period the truth
that the conditions of life and business in this

country, especially those connected with universal suffrage, involve some difficult problems, and some serious disadvantages for those who work for wages.

I have here presented as many of the principal facts of this man's life and work as I am able to embody in a paper of no greater length. A master of fiction could portray an ideal character, and supply more dramatic incidents. This account is merely true. It describes the life of a quiet, humane gentleman, — one who has been most useful to his fellows, who has aided in the development of whole regions of our country, and who, I am sure, never knowingly harmed any human being. And yet this man, according to the teaching of those who pretend to be the best friends of the laboring man, is an enemy to society, an oppressor of the poor and of all who toil. He has a beautiful home, with pictures, flowers, books, scientific collections and instruments. But it is urged that my friend has no right to these possessions, that they are the evidences and proceeds of injustice, because he is a capitalist, because he does not labor with his hands. Yet he has provided and directed remunerative labor for an army of men who had not ability or opportunity to provide it for themselves. He has trained hundreds of these men till they were able in their turn to provide work for others. As I have heard the abuse and execration which unreasoning partisans have heaped upon all capitalists, I have wished to tell the story of some lives that I have known. I am well assured that wise teaching — the truth — respecting the relations between capital and labor, or rather those between capitalists and laborers, is still as important and necessary as before the recent political defeat of some of the disorganizing elements and tendencies in our society. We shall be exposed to similar dangers and difficulties while so large a proportion of the whole people retain the qualities of mind and thought which are the real source of our perils. We cannot expect speedily to suppress or root out these evils; we can only hope to maintain our ground against them, and gradually to expel them by wise vigilance and by unhesitating acceptance of the responsibility of propagating knowledge and true culture.

My friend has always clearly understood the necessity of honestly paying the debts of the nation which were incurred during the war, and he thinks that if our people could have been wise enough to be strictly honest in matters of national finance and currency, we might have escaped something of the paralysis of business and industry from which we have recently suffered. He laments the madness of the workingmen in demanding irredeemable paper money, but thinks that the cultivated people and business men of the nation should understand that, if there is great disturbance and depression of industry in the country, and particularly if many people are for some time out of employment, some such popular

madness is almost certain to arise. He believes
there may still be danger and difficulty before us
in matters of national finance, on account of the
clumsy and unnecessary silver legislation, and
fears that the fluctuating value of silver may be
an embarrassing element in the problem of resumption of specie payments. I find that most
of the business men of my acquaintance distrust
the effect of a double standard of value, and believe the present experiment of a bi-metallic cur-
reney can end only in disaster; but they fancy
it is inevitable that we shall try many foolish experiments, and that we may as well try this one
now. My friend thinks the American people will
be obliged to learn that the yard-stick has been
made for some time, and its length established,
and that for all honest men it is thirty-six inches
long; that there are one hundred cents in a real
dollar; and that the hope even of pecuniary gain
from schemes of readjustment, repudiation, and
debasing the currency is an illusion. All en-
deavors to obtain something for nothing he regards
as stupid and foolish; fairness and integrity being
in his estimation a kind of capital without which
success in business is impossible. This gentleman
never engages in electioneering, and does not purposely influence those who are in his employ; but
the facts of his life, such as I have here described,
have profoundly impressed many of the working
people about him, and the intellectual conditions
of the region where he lives are in consequence

comparatively unfavorable for the development of hostility to capitalists, although the workingmen constitute so large a proportion of the population.

It might be instructive to compare this life with the course of any one of the politicians who denounce capitalists with such vehement bitterness. I asked my friend not long ago if he had not lost much money by trusting dishonest or incompetent men. He replied that he had had such losses, adding, " But every kind of business has its risks, and I should probably have had greater losses if I had invested in stocks or mortgages in the usual way." He said that such a course would have given him far less labor, care, and anxiety than the one he has followed. In times of great depression he has felt burdened and anxious on account of the difficulty of providing labor for his people ; and has often kept them employed for a long time when nothing could be sold for as much as it cost. He holds that when laborers are idle, capital always declines in value. He thinks the first step toward improvement in times of great depression is for workmen to live on as little as possible, and for capitalists to employ as much labor as they can. Let the laborers live savingly, and the capitalists be content with small profits.

STUDY OF A NEW ENGLAND FACTORY TOWN.

THE place has about fifty thousand inhabitants. It has one great industrial occupation, the making of cotton cloth of various kinds. There are more than forty mills used for this manufacture, — great buildings, some of them hundreds of feet in length, and six stories high ; most of them are of granite, but a few are of brick. They do not occupy any particular region in the city, but are found in nearly every part of it, — in the central squares and principal business streets, and even in those in which the most substantial and elegant dwellings are situated, as well as in the poorer quarters and in the suburbs.

I visited the place recently, and saw something of the life of the operatives and of other portions of the population. Various friends had offered me letters of introduction to prominent citizens and owners of the mills ; but I have long been aware that when one wishes to see things directly, and for himself, introductions are not always helpful. They are apt to commit an observer to certain lines and methods of investigation, and they necessitate the adoption, at the outset, of some plan of operations ; and this, whether it is ad-

hered to or discarded, is commonly a disadvan-
tage. A man who is capable of making valuable
observations of the life around him can usually
obtain access to all those persons who possess
knowledge or information which is essential to his
objects ; and he can do this most successfully by
making his plans as he goes on, — that is, by leaving himself free to adapt his methods, at every
step, to circumstances and conditions which could
not possibly be foreseen.

I employed one day in leisurely sauntering
about the city, in the course of which I saw
nearly all its streets and by-ways, its nooks and
out-of-the-way corners. During the day the noise
of the machinery of the mills fills the air of the
whole city with a muffled humming sound, which
is not unmusical, but rather soft and dreamy ; inside of the mills the shrill buzz and clatter are
at first rather painful to unaccustomed ears. In
the evening I saw the mill people on their way
to their homes. When I walked in the direction
opposite to theirs, so as to meet them and see
their faces, I noted that they all regarded me with
alert, searching glances, and they were plainly
at once aware that I was a stranger. A group
of children came first, laughing and chattering.
They were about twelve or fourteen years old.
One of the girls gave me a critical look, and remarked to her companions, " He 's a detective." I
heard that exclamation many times during the
first few days of my sojourn, but the operatives

soon recognized me everywhere. I often walked
in the same direction with them, going a little
more slowly than they, so as to hear their talk.
It did not differ greatly from that of young people of about the same age of any class with which
I am acquainted : " what Jane said about you ; "
" what Ned told Delia Smith ; " and animated
remarks about the " new things " which some of
the girls had bought lately, with grave talk of the
sickness of some of their companions ; all this
accompanied and interrupted by frequent careless,
noisy laughter. It was rather pleasant and encouraging. The young people of the mills appeared to be very much like other young people
when in a crowd together in the street.

When I inquired at the hotels whether one
could see the mills, the answer was, " Yes, most
of them ; but at a few of the largest the rules for-
bid the admission of visitors. The officers are
very strict, and if you are a stranger you cannot
go in." In the shops and business houses which
various errands led me to visit, and in which I
always met gentlemen who were ready to talk
about the trade and manufactures of their city,
this information about the mills from which visitors were excluded was often repeated, and the
same mills were always named. I therefore decided to begin by looking through the places
which were thus reported to be difficult of access.
I encountered no obstacle anywhere that was not
easily surmounted. I passed through more than

half a dozen of the largest mills, inspecting all the processes and details of the manufacture, from the boiler room in the cellar, where the smooth, resistless swing of the gigantic Corliss engines made 'one feel as if he were watching the motion of a planet in its path, to the enormous tubs of sizing, high up in the attic.

In all the mills which I visited, far more than half the operatives were girls and women. I saw very few children who appeared to be under twelve years of age, though I heard much criticism, among some of my new acquaintances in the city, of the cruelty of the laws and usages relating to the employment of young children in the mills. As to nationality or descent, the English, Scotch, and Irish operatives, with their children born here, constitute the most numerous classes, but there are also many French Canadians. I had often heard and read the assertion that very few Americans, or, more strictly, descendants of American families, now work in the mills. But I found among the operatives a considerable proportion of young women who are the children of families that have lived in this country for one hundred and fifty or two hundred years, and I have since learned that the same thing is true of several other factory towns.

All the mill people looked as if they had enough to eat, but some of them showed in their faces indications of the effects of poor cookery. Some had the peculiar look which comes from living in impure air, and this result is produced chiefly, as I was convinced by what I saw in the mills and in the homes of the people, by the foulness of the air in the rooms in which the operatives eat and sleep. In many, probably in most, of their homes the cooking is done in the "sitting-room;" that is, the apartment in which the members of the family pass the evening together until bed-time. The cost of fuel is one of the principal expenditures and burdens of the household, and economy in its use is one of the most important means of saving; so the room is kept closely shut to prevent the escape of heat and the entrance of cold air from the outside. The impurity of the air in these rooms during cold weather is very great, and this is one of the most unwholesome features of the life of the operatives.

The cotton is brought to the mills in the bale, "just as it comes from the fields in Indiana, or wherever it grows," as an obliging overseer in one of the largest mills explained to me, and all the processes of picking, cleaning, carding, spinning, weaving, dressing, and finishing are performed in the same building. Nearly all this work is done by machinery, and the labor of the operatives consists almost entirely in attendance upon the machinery. There are a few things, such as the drawing of the threads of the warp through the "harness," which are done with the fingers, but the wonderful capabilities of the machines leave very few things to be done by human

11

hands. Many of the looms are so constructed that they stop at once if a thread breaks, and do not go on till it is mended. Each girl tends four, five, or six looms. A few of the most skillful can manage eight looms each, as many as the best hands among the men.

There is not much work that requires great muscular strength or exertion, not much lifting or handling heavy materials or articles of any kind. Most of it requires alertness and exactness of attention, the concentration of the faculties and their constant application to the processes going on under one's hand, rather than severe muscular effort. Such work usually exhausts the nervous vitality quite as rapidly as many occupations which appear to be more difficult and toilsome. Most of the operatives are necessarily on their feet nearly all the time, and this feature of their work has an unfavorable effect upon the health of the women and girls. They all appear to be tired at the end of their day's toil, though I saw no signs of extreme weariness or exhaustion. It is very hard for any one who is not well, or who is " nervous " and sensitive. The noise of the machinery then becomes insufferably irritating and torturing.

No part of the work in the mills appeared to me so severe, or so unwholesome, for girls and women as is the toil of those who run sewing-machines in city shops; yet it is work which requires good health and high average vitality. The high temperature which is necessary for some of the

processes of cotton manufacture renders the operatives specially liable, during the winter, to injury
by taking cold when they pass into the open air,
unless they use some precautions against it by
putting on extra clothing when they leave the
mills. But I observed that most of them were
careless in this respect, though not more so, probably, than is usual among the pupils of the high-
schools in every part of our country. I noted considerable coughing, and some complained of sore
throats. In several departments of a mill the air
is always filled by fine flying fibres and particles of
cotton. Some of these are drawn into the lungs,
and this produces injurious effects. When the
lungs are at all sensitive or inclined to disease, this
dust increases the irritation. Even for persons
who are strong and well it is of course unwholesome, and it probably causes greater injury to
health than any other feature or condition of mill
work.

A group or company of the young people of the
mills, when approached by a stranger, always exhibits the peculiar instinctive shrinking and drawing together for self-defense which is shown by
wild animals in similar circumstances. In the
mill people it is a feeling of distrust, suspicion,
and hostility regarding all who do not belong to
their class. The first question asked of a stranger
is always, " Do you wish to get work in the
mill ? " Of course I was simply a stranger, who
wished to see the mills and the work which was

done in them. During the hour at noon, when the machinery is at rest, is a favorable time for forming some acquaintance with the operatives. Many of them have brought their dinner with them, and they eat it sitting on the floor, or standing in groups together. One scarcely knows when or how the eating is done in some of these little companies, for the talk and chatter and laughter are incessant. The presence of a stranger is at first a restraint, and excites their caution when he approaches or addresses them. Unless a man knows how to penetrate and disarm this reserve, he will learn little from them of their thought or life. They soon became merry and communicative with me. Some of the younger girls were then inclined to be forward and impudent, but they were checked and controlled by the older ones.

The girls and young women in the mills "learn to take care of themselves," to use a phrase which one often hears among them ; that is, they are not at all ignorant of evil or vice. They know what are the dangers that beset and threaten young girls in their circumstances, among men many of whom are coarse and sensual. In such conditions the delicacy and modesty of thought, deportment, and speech which are so precious and lovely in the character of young women are almost impossible, and we have no right to require or expect them. But these girls are not so liable to be led into actual vice or immorality as are some of the pupils in our Sunday-schools, whose very ignorance of evil, and of the need of avoiding or resisting it, sometimes exposes them to temptation unwarned and unprepared. The mill girls are familiar with coarse and vile language, and can hear it unabashed and without blushing; they can answer in like terms. But these facts are not, in their case, marks of extreme depravity or immorality. They afford no evidence of unchastity. I do not believe that this vice prevails to any considerable extent among the young women of the mills. Some of the older women, especially among the English and Irish, have not always been successful in self-protection, or in repelling temptation, as one can plainly see. But there is, as I am thoroughly convinced, far less of sexual vice among the factory operatives than is usually attributed to them. I am certain that working-people in general, of both sexes, are more pure and free from this vice than most moralists and clergymen think them. Their toil represses passion. Their time is filled by their regular occupations, and they have little leisure for vicious thoughts, for nourishing mischievous and profligate desires. It is among idle men and women that this evil finds most of its recruits. No system of morals or of religious culture has yet been devised which provides any effective safeguard against licentiousness for those who are exempt from toil.

In studying the life of any class of people, an observer soon distinguishes the persons who can be of use to him, who represent or possess something which he wishes to learn or understand. When I had found several men and women who could thus be of service to me, the next step was to visit their homes, which I did upon their invitation. I saw their food and their methods of preparing it, examined the books and papers which they read, and listened to their accounts of their own life and work and experience.

There are but few " tenement houses " in this place owned by the mill proprietors. Most of the operatives find homes or apartments wherever they prefer, and many of them live in small buildings where there are only two or three families under the same roof. I think this much better than the system of large tenement houses, unless these could be superior in design and arrangement to the buildings of this class which are ordinarily found in American cities. There are, however, a few large buildings here belonging to the mill owners, and each is occupied by a large number of families. I examined two or three of them, and am compelled to say that their construction is not what it should be. In some cases the cellars are not properly secured against the ingress of surface water, and the water-closets are inadequate and unsuitable. The city government should give this matter immediate attention. The tenants should be required by the proprietors to keep the yards surrounding these houses in a more wholesome and cleanly condition than that in which I found them.

The cookery in the homes of the operatives, if judged by what I saw and learned in several families, is not usually very good. They fry too much of their food, and many do not know how to extract the nutritive elements from beef-bones by long boiling. They throw out to their dogs what would give them the basis for a valuable and delicious soup. (The operatives keep a great many dogs, as is the custom among poor people generally, in this country.) If the women had sufficient knowledge in regard to the best methods of preparing it, they could have better food and more of it without additional expense. Much good might be done by an arrangement for instructing these women and girls in economical methods of preparing wholesome and appetizing food. Perhaps the good women of the city who possess the advantages of wealth and culture can do something to aid their less fortunate sisters among the operatives in this matter.

The young people of the mills generally read the story papers, published (most of them) in New York city, and devoted to interminably "continued" narratives, of which there are always three or four in process of publication in each paper. I have read some of these stories. They have usually no very distinct educational quality or tendency, good or bad. They are simply stories, — vapid, silly, turgid, and incoherent. As the robber-heroes are mostly grand-looking fellows, and all the ladies have white hands and splendid at-

tire, it may be that some of the readers find hard
work more distasteful because of their acquaintance with the gorgeous idlers and thieves, who, in
these fictions are always so much more fortunate
than the people who are honest and industrious.
But usually, as I am convinced by much observation, the only effect of this kind of reading is that
it serves " to pass away the time," by supplying
a kind of entertainment, a stimulus or opiate for
the mind, and that these people resort to it and
feel a necessity for it in much the same way that
others feel they must have whisky or opium.
The reading is a narcotic, but it is less pernicious
than those just named.

Many hundreds of the older operatives, especially foreigners, of two or three nationalities, were
reading a paper which is devoted to the liberation
of the working-people of America.   Its principal
literary attraction at this time was a very long
serial story of the overthrow of the republic in
1880.   This is written as if the events which form
the subject of the narrative had already occurred.
It introduces General Grant as dictator, and describes elaborately the character and effects of the
terrible despotism which he establishes, in that
year, upon the ruins of popular government.   He
"suppresses Congress," seizes New York city at
the head of an armed force and by the assistance
of the capitalists or " money power " of the country, and is about to make himself emperor, when
the working-people rise in arms, under the direc-

tion of a nameless leader, " a man with the executive intellect of Cæsar, Napoleon, and Bismarck, and the lofty impulses of Leonidas, Cincinnatus, and Washington." (To continue the description of this personage, " he was a man of huge bulk and brawn. His head was the size and shape of Daniel Webster's, whom he greatly resembled, except in being of the blonde type. His awful gray eyes had a power in them far beyond that of the orbs of the indolent Webster.")

The workingmen, soldiers of the new revolution, are instructed by this hero to supply their own needs from the abundant stores of their neighbors, giving them receipts in the name of the revolution for the property thus forcibly appropriated. They accordingly seize the national banks, and help themselves to as much money as they desire. This story was read with deep interest by many of the older operatives, especially those who were interested in labor reform. The paper containing it prints each week a declaration of principles, which affirms that the government should hold all the land of the nation ; that it should be without price (the free use of as much of it as he can cultivate being secured to every man) ; that ground rents of towns and cities should be controlled by government ; that gold and silver should be demonetized, and that in their stead absolute paper money should be issued by the government ; that interest on money should be forbidden ; that all mines, railroads, and highways should be owned and controlled by the government; that the government ought not to interfere for the collection of debts between individuals, but that the payment of debts should be left entirely to the honor of the debtor. There should be an income tax on all incomes above one thousand dollars, growing heavier for larger sums. Eight hours' labor should be a legal day's work, and the senate of the United States should be abolished. Recently the paper has devoted much space to the advocacy of " the right of the people to free travel: " the government should own the railroads, and tax capitalists to obtain means for operating them, and people who do not wish to pay fares should be permitted to ride free. This paper has a large circulation among operatives, miners, and city mechanics, in nearly all parts of the country. It is a large sheet, and is conducted with much ability. It always contains two or three serial stories by popular writers, which are designed to " float " the heavier articles devoted to the propagation of the doctrines of the agitators, who seek to establish a universal, international sovereignty of workingmen upon principles and methods which contradict and oppose every essential of civilization. The tone and spirit of the paper are indescribably bitter, and expressive of intense hostility against the possessors of property and culture. It represents capitalists as a class of cruel and inhuman oppressors, and instructs the working-people that the time is at hand for them to seize the rights of which they have been so long deprived. All its teaching is opposed to the spirit and principle of nationality, and tends, so far as it has any effect, to produce social and political disintegration.

There is a labor-reform newspaper published in this city of mills, and I had much conversation with the editor. He thinks the mill owners and capitalists of the city are thoroughly selfish and heartless ; that they have no regard for the interests or welfare of the operatives, and care only to obtain the greatest possible amount of labor from them for the least possible pay. He was engaged, when I saw him, in the promotion of a movement having for its object the reduction of the hours of labor in the mills. The legal day's work is now ten hours, but my friend the editor informed me that the mill agents often disregard the law and work the hands ten and a half, and even eleven hours per day. He said that the largest mill in the city was run nearly seventy hours one week, and that the agent of this mill was " determined to be king of devils."

I asked the editor what change he regarded as, at present, most important and necessary for the emancipation of labor and the improvement of the condition of the working-people ; and he replied, " The next great step is the reduction of the hours of labor."

" What should be the length of a day's work ? "

" We are working now to obtain more stringent legislation against running the mills more than ten hours, but six hours a day would be enough for people to work."

I asked him if he could give me any information regarding the amount of deposits by operatives in the savings-banks of the city. This is his reply, in a note which he kindly sent me not long ago, and which is now before me : " I have no exact means of stating the precise amount, but it is practically nothing. There is no city where the operatives own fewer bank-books than here. The operatives of this city are very poor indeed, perhaps no place poorer, and the per cent. who own their homes is a great deal smaller. Factory life has almost reached serfdom."

I thought my friend a well-meaning, sincere man, but extreme in his bitterness against capitalists. He could give me little information regarding the most important features of the life of the operatives of his city, but I am grateful to him for the opportunity for acquaintance with his opinions and the aims of his fellow-reformers.

I am obliged to say that I found few signs of interest among the work people in reforms of any kind. Most of them appeared to be entirely indifferent to such matters, and to political subjects in general. But there is a considerable number of men, especially among the spinners, who are discontented under what they deem tyranny and oppression on the part of the mill owners and agents. These operatives have an organization, or society, for the promotion of their aims, and they employ a secretary with a salary sufficient to enable him to devote his time to their interests. I met this secretary, and had a long conversation with him. He is a foreigner, and seemed a very good-natured fellow. He thought that in cases of dissatisfaction on the part of the operatives, the employers were usually ready to hear and consider any statement which the working-people might wish to present through a committee of their own choosing. He appeared to regard the owners and agents as reasonable men, who were disposed to deal justly with the laborers ; and I thought that he, more than any other of the reformers whom I met, understood that both capitalists and laborers in this country are suffering from the operation of causes which no legislation or reform could at once remove.

The operatives are paid by the piece, and not by the day or hour; that is, it is the quantity of goods manufactured, and not the amount of time employed, which determines the amount of wages paid. The reformers complained that when a new mill is opened the agent stimulates the operatives to the highest possible performance and production for the first few days, and then adjusts the wages-rate upon the basis of what the best hands have thus been able to do for a short time. As only a few operatives are capable of such a pace, and even they cannot maintain it permanently, the arrangement has the effect of establishing a low rate of wages. (That is, if we rep-

resent by one hundred the amount of work performed in a day by the best hands when spurred
to unusual activity, the average daily performance
will not rise above eighty-five or ninety; but the
amount of pay is regulated upon the assumption
that the average daily work will reach one hundred.)

The reformers thought the average pay of the
operatives of the city, at the time of my visit, was
considerably less than one dollar per day for "full
hands," that is, for those who can do a full day's
work ; but the mill owners and agents assured me
that the average pay was above one dollar per
day. I visited the agents and managers of several
of the largest mills, and asked them for their view
of the condition of the operatives and of the situation and prospects of the cotton manufacture
in the city. They answered my inquiries with
ready, quiet courtesy. Here is the substance of
the notes which I made as we talked : —

" The women weavers are paid a little more
than one dollar per day. Any boy of thirteen or
fourteen years old can make two dollars and a
half per week. Operatives pay for rent, for four
rooms, from three and a half dollars to six dollars per month. The owners and managers are
satisfied with the ten-hour law, and do not think
any additional legislation necessary (in this State)
for the proper regulation of the relations between
capital and labor, or the working-people and their
employers. We prefer ten hours per day, but as

the machinery is run by steam-power we have to start it a little before the hour, and some of the hands always go to work at once, in order to add a little to the day's production, and so to their wages. At present rates of pay, the average operatives can save something from their wages. If we compare the cost of living and wages of the times before the war, say in 1860, with the cost of living and wages now, we shall find that operatives are better paid now than they were then. All of us, operatives and employers, have lived more extravagantly since the war than ever before. All wars make waste, and we are all of us suffering from the consequences of the waste caused by our civil war, and especially by the unwise expenditure of money since 1865. When wages were very high, a few years ago, the operatives wasted nearly all that they received. Few of them saved anything. We must all learn and practice economy. Many people who are regarded as being rich are living more carefully and economically than most of the working-people, because they have more foresight and a clearer understanding of the absolute necessity of keeping their expenditures within their income.

" The corporations do not own one fourth of the tenements or dwellings occupied by the operatives. It is for the interest of the capitalists that the operatives should own the houses they live in, and that as many as possible should have homes of their own. The capitalists and mill

owners of the city all wish the operatives to buy
land and build houses, and are always ready to
sell them land at low rates, and to allow as much
time for the payment as the purchasers desire.
Many of the operatives in the largest mill, and
some in all of them, have thus come into possession of comfortable homes. A man and his wife
came into one of the mills, a few years ago, from
a manufacturing town in England. They were
then about fifty years old, and had never been
able to have meat on their table except when now
and then the man caught a hare. They were
industrious and economical, saved money, and
bought a piece of ground. A year or two ago
they built a four-tenement house (a house with
suites of rooms for four families). They occupy
one and let the three others to tenants, and are
living in comfort and happiness.

" For several years the mills have been run in
the interest of the operatives. Probably not more
than one fourth of the mills in the city can pay
any dividends during the current year. The capital invested in the mills amounts to nearly thirty
millions of dollars; and for several years the
profits upon these investments have not equaled
one half of the lowest rates of interest paid by
the savings-banks of the country. If the ideas
or principles of the trades-unions could be carried
out, half the mills would be bankrupt in ten years.
The intelligence of the laboring people is increasing; we hope so, at any rate. A few wrong-

headed and impracticable men wish to make mischief. In all cases of dissatisfaction on the part of operatives if they appoint a committee to meet the managers, everything can be amicably arranged ; but a few agitators do whatever they can to produce discontent among the working-people, and to disturb the relations between them and their employers. One of the labor reformers bought a share or two of the stock of one of the largest mills, in order to gain admission to the meetings of the stockholders. Then he constantly reported the proceedings of these meetings to the trades-union of which he was a member, and used the knowledge he had obtained relative to the affairs of the mill corporation as a basis for perpetual complaint and agitation among the operatives."

The capitalists and mill owners of the city with whom I conversed attributed the prevailing depression of business and industry in large measure to the waste of capital necessarily produced by our civil war, and in still greater degree to the extravagance of expenditure which was so general among our people a few years ago. They thought that the principal means of recovery must be economy and wisdom in expenditure; that capitalists and employers have come to understand this necessity more fully than the operatives do, as a class; and that those who belong to the capitalist class are at present really more saving and economical in their methods of living than the operatives.

I was greatly interested in learning about the amusements or diversions of the mill people. My first step was to ask a great many of the young women what they did in the evening, after working hours were over. The French Canadian girls, who are Catholics, nearly all replied, " We stay at home. We have to sew, and mend our clothes, and wash them. We do not know anybody, and so we have no place to go in the evening." At times the answer was, " My mother " or " my sister will not let me go out." Most of the other young women said, " Oh, we go out with our fellers, and with some of the other girls." " And where do you go ? " " Oh, along the streets, down town ; to the post-office, or the candy-store, if the boys will shout." " If they will shout, — what is that ? " " Oh, don't you know ? Why, that means if they will treat, — if they will buy some candy for us." " And do you drink something, too ? " To this the younger women always answered, " No, we don't drink anything, unless it's soda-water, sometimes, in warm weather." But they usually pointed to some older companion, and said, " She drinks, — she drinks beer." Then the woman thus spoken of would laugh, and toss her head, and say, " Ain't you goin' to shout ? " And when I met the same group in the street in the evening, the question would be repeated, with a smile of recognition.

I do not think these girls and younger women have usually any habitual amusement, except this walking out with their friends which I have just mentioned. Once or twice during the winter many of them go to a ball. To go more frequently would be regarded by their own class as an extravagance, as an indication of unsteadiness and a tendency to dissipation. I found many young people in the mills who " belonged," as they said, to the Methodist church, and some who were Baptists. Probably there were, among the operatives, members of other religious societies, but I did not happen to meet them.

The young people whom I have thus far been describing appeared to be rather steady and well-behaved. They looked and acted as if they kept good hours, and had no marks of anything wild or irregular about them. But I saw others, both young men and women, whom I knew at once to be of a different type. Every class, every type of character, has a rhythm of its own, which runs through all bodily movements, through the tones of the voice; which is accented in glances and changes of expression, and is revealed in all spontaneous mental action. I knew that some of these young people would have other amusements than those I have described. I did not think it wise to ask any of them how they passed their evenings. I thought there might be better ways of acquiring this knowledge.

I had observed in various parts of the city such

signs as " Harmony Hall," " The Avon Arms,"
" St. George's Hall," etc. I sauntered into one
of these places, one evening, about nine o'clock.
It was on the second floor, and was reached by
an open stair-way running up from the street. I
found a hall about fifty feet long and twenty-five
wide. At one end was a bar for the sale of liquors, and at the other a curtained recess and a
small stage or platform elevated two or three steps
from the floor. There were about fifty persons present, grouped around eight or ten tables. About
one fourth of them were young women. Some
of the young men were smoking. There were
glasses on the tables, and some of the young people were drinking beer. As I went up the stairs,
I heard the clang of a piano much out of tune and
the clapping of hands, and a young man was just
descending from the stage, while he smiled and
bowed in acknowledgment of the applause. He
sat down with one of the groups nearest the stage,
and some one at the table called for " four beers."
The four glasses were taken away by a pleasant-
looking English girl, and brought back filled.
There were similar requests from various parts of
the room, and after she had responded to them
the young waitress approached the place where I
sat alone, and civilly inquired, " Is there anything
you wish for ? " I gave her an order that would
bring her back to my table now and then.

When most of the glasses had been emptied
once or twice, some one said, quietly, " Mr. Lee

will oblige," and there was a general clapping of hands. A young Englishman ascended the stage, and sang, in tolerable accord with the weary, protesting piano, a melancholy song about a sailor lover who sailed away from his mistress and never returned. Both hearts were true : one lies " in his long, last sleep, a thousand fathoms deep, where the wild monsoons do sweep " forever above his rest; the other " watched her life away, looking seaward o'er the bay," from a New England hill-top, and hoping to the end for one who came no more. At the close there was more applause and more beer, and for some time busy, chattering talk. There was nothing loud or boisterous. One of the girls, who was a little tipsy, came across the room, in a rather demonstrative way, and asked me if I was not " going to shout ; " but a young man at the table she had left reproved her sharply, and one of the young women from the same company came over and led her back to her place.

By this time I had noted most of those present as persons whom I had met before, in the mills and on the streets. They were nearly all operatives, or had at some time belonged to that class. But I observed at one of the tables, with half a dozen young men and women around him, a young colored man whom I had never seen until now. He was more silent than any other member of the company, but was evidently the object of general attention and respect. He was the only

person of his color in the hall, but was plainly
as welcome there as any one. He seemed ob-
viously superior to his neighbors, and I was interested at once, and felt that I must know something about him. Presently there was another
invitation to the stage, and when the young colored man rose to comply with it there was unusually hearty applause. He sang one song after
another till he seemed tired, but the audience was
still impatient for more. The songs were of many
kinds, comic, sentimental, pathetic, and silly. One
had these stanzas : —

> "Sampson was a strong man,
>   He was not counted lazy;
> He took the jaw-bone of a shark
>   And slewed the gates of Gazy.

> "It rained forty days and forty nights
>   Exactly by the countin',
> And landed Noah and his ark
>   On the Alleghany mountain."

When he sang "I got a mammy in the promised
land," with a strange, wailing refrain, the English
waiter-girl, who was sitting at my table, wiped
her eyes with her apron, and everybody was very
quiet. He sang and acted with a kind of sup-
pressed intensity of manner and expression, and
I thought that to him the dusty hall and its somewhat squalid appointments had given place to
a grand theatre, thronged by an admiring, applauding audience. He seemed rapt and inspired.
His face was black, and the features African in
type, but not at all repulsive or unpleasant. When

he left the stage, I sent the waiter-girl to tell him I wished to see him. He came down the hall with a dignified courtesy of manner; we were introduced, and had a little conversation. I found him very intelligent. He talked well, but quietly and deliberately. His speech was that of cultivated New England people, and had none of the peculiarities which usually mark the language and utterance of colored persons.

It would not do to show too much curiosity or interest there, as this was my first visit to the hall; but I arranged to meet my colored friend next day, and took my leave, assured of a welcome there whenever I might return. I visited half a dozen similar places before midnight. They were all much alike. I spent several hours, at various times, in these music halls, calling sometimes in the afternoon, because the attendants had more time then than in the evening. Some of them had stories to tell which I wished to hear, but I had to wait till I had established such relations between us as would inspire them with the willingness to talk to me.

All the attendants at these places had worked in the mills. The young man who plays the piano is usually paid four or five dollars per week, besides his board. The young men who sing receive one dollar per night, but most of them board themselves. The real business at all these places is the sale of liquor. They all keep cigars, and most of them have pies and a few other articles

of food, but the profits come from the drinking.
The piano, the singing, and recitations attract and
entertain visitors.   These resorts are sustained almost entirely by the operatives, besides a great
many other places where there is no music or entertainment of any kind, except the drink.   At
the city clerk's office I learned from the official
records that there are in the city two hundred
and fifty-seven houses licensed to sell liquors, and
many of the leading citizens expressed the opinion that the unlicensed drinking places (where
liquor is sold unlawfully) were at least equal in
number.   Last year there were 5,400 voters in the
city; so there was a licensed drinking saloon for
every twenty-one voters.   The city's revenue from
these licenses last year was $38,782.   This large
sum, and a great deal besides, the liquor dealers
received from the working-people, — a very large
proportion of it from the mill hands.   At one of
these music halls the woman in charge informed
me that "the expenses of the establishment"
averaged two hundred dollars per month, and I
visited several places which did a much larger
business than this one.

The editor of the labor-reform newspaper told
me that the most usual course for a man who for
any reason falls out of the ranks of mill workers
(if he loses his place by sickness, or is discharged)
is the opening of a liquor saloon or drinking place.
He takes up this business for a living and rarely
quits it for any other occupation.   At first, he

buys a very small stock, — a keg of beer, or a few gallons of low-grade whisky. He hires a little corner or closet in some shop or basement, or he begins in his own cellar, and is soon able to lay in a larger and more varied supply. After much observation and study of the subject in most of the States of our country, I believe there is no other kind of business or employment which can be entered upon or engaged in with so little capital, or which will yield so large a return in proportion to the amount invested. There is greater profit and less risk of loss than in any other occupation which is open to so many people. Its principal support comes from the classes engaged in manual labor. Many men will buy intoxicating liquors when they and their families are suffering for food. Whatever degree of poverty may prevail among the working-people, those who sell liquor to them still find the business profitable. The great causes of the drinking habit among the working-people are poor cookery, living in impure air, and the lack of any dramatic entertainment or amusement for their evenings or times of leisure.

I met the young colored man several times, and found him a person to give one a sad kind of interest in him. He was just then doing more to amuse and entertain the mill people than any one else in the city, so I gave a little time to conversation with him. I like average and ordinary men and women best, and have not commonly found what is unusual or extraordinary in human life or character best worth study or acquaintance. But this man was not precisely what I was looking for. On one occasion I asked him who was the author of a song he had just sung. Looking at me keenly, he asked, "Do you like it?" "Yes," I said; "it is simple and tender and natural." "Well," he replied, "it is mine, such as it is." "Do you mean that you wrote the words?" "Yes, the words and the music." "Have you written others?" "Oh, yes; I have quite an income from my songs." "Where are they published?" He gave me the name of a well-known music-publishing house in Boston, and when I came home I ordered specimens of my friend's compositions. They were sent to me, and I found everything as he had told me.

I asked him if he had been singing at these places in the city very long. "Nearly a year," he replied; and then he told me that his business was negro minstrelsy and theatricals. He had traveled with the principal companies in this country, and had a permanent engagement at a good salary. But about a year ago his mother died. He was greatly attached to her, was with her in her last illness, and was "too heart-broken to be making money. I did not feel like acting, and thought it would show more respect to my mother, if she knows about it, if I did not appear in public for a year. I sing a little in this private way to accommodate my friends here, and because it is not good to be doing nothing." He acknowledged that he drank too much, and that his life was not what it should be. I asked him if anybody had ever encouraged him to cultivate his mind and make a man of himself. "No," said he; "the only encouragement anybody ever gave me was, ' Bill, go another dollar on this l'" But many people would probably find this man's story more interesting if it were not true.

At the principal hotel I met many salesmen and book-keepers from the shops and stores of the city, and when there was opportunity I sometimes made inquiries regarding the mill people, — their character and ways of living. These gentlemen always appeared to be surprised that I should be interested about the operatives, or suppose there was anything in their life that was worthy of attention. At one time there was considerable excitement among my friends at the hotel, on account of the announcement that a certain " celebrated star troupe " of actors would appear " for one night only " at the Academy of Music. It was to be a " variety entertainment," to comprise a play in two acts, songs, dances, a trapeze performance, etc., — all of the very highest character. My companions at the table courteously advised me to go. It would be a good opportunity to see the people of the city, as the attendance would be very large. " Will the mill people be there ? " I inquired. " Oh, no [with impatience] ; they are not capable of appreciating anything of this kind. They have their own low amusements, but this is first-class." I went. The house was filled with well-dressed people of both sexes. The feature of the entertainment which was most to the mind of the audience was a song. A rather pretty girl came out in spangled tights, and sang half a dozen stanzas with this refrain : —

> "So, boys, keep away from the girls, I say,
>   And give them plenty of room ;
> For when you are wed they will bang till you 're dead
>   With the bald-headed end of a broom."

This was " received with great enthusiasm," as the play-bills said it would be, and was encored again and again. I looked around over the applauding multitude; the mill people were not there.

The mills were running on full time, and were worked to their utmost capacity, with all the hands the machinery would employ. They require about fifteen thousand hands. But there were, as I judged from all I could learn about the matter, between fifteen hundred and two thousand persons of the operative class in the city in excess of the number which the mills could employ. These were destitute of work, except when, now and then, the temporary illness of some hand left a place vacant, and so gave the opportunity of work to one of these superfluous laborers for a day or two. There was much hardship among these people. Many had families, and their children suffered for food. In some of the worst cases the city gave assistance; the labor unions sustained others, in part; and neighborly kindness among the operatives was more helpful than either. The labor-reform agitation, in all its stages, from vague discontent to violent denunciation, was reinforced and sustained chiefly by the presence of this unemployed class. Their life was a daily struggle against the inevitable, — a long and useless waiting for what could not come. Every morning some hundreds of these seekers after employment presented themselves at the doors of the mills, in the hope, almost always a vain one, that a few of them might be wanted.

The overseers at the mills kindly allowed persons seeking work to put down their names in application for the opportunity of filling vacancies when they should occur. In visiting one of these unemployed families, I saw a fine-looking, capable young man, who had been idle for months. His name was on the list at one of the principal mills, but there were twenty-eight names before his, and it was not probable that his turn would ever come. This young man bears a well-known name, and his ancestors have lived in the State more than two hundred years. The presence of so large a number of superfluous hands in any place is a matter of grave importance. There were too many laborers there already, but every day there were new arrivals from other manufacturing towns. Some, on learning that the mills were crowded, resumed their quest in new directions. Others

had not means to go farther, and remained to
swell the number of the unemployed and discontented. Is it impossible to devise some plan which
would prevent this migration of crowds of laborers to places where there is no demand for labor
and no prospect of their finding employment?
We already map the course of the winds and the
state of the weather for the whole country each
day. Would it be much more difficult to map the
state of the labor market for the whole country
every week or every month, or less valuable in its
results? The impotence of society in the presence
of such evils is more apparent than real.

I found several large Catholic temperance societies among the mill people. They were working
vigorously and with excellent effect. The Catholic Church is doing more than any other, I think.
for the moral guidance and improvement of the
operatives. The Methodist Church comes next,
and its work is important and salutary. I saw
evidences, now and then, among the young Methodist converts, of strong sectarian feeling, a dispo-
sitiou to employ social pressure as a means of increasing the influence of the church. As this was,
under the circumstances, a sign of earnestness and
vitality, it was a less evil than indifference. The
Baptist Church has also a considerable share in
the religious culture of the mill people; and it is
probable that other religious bodies, besides those
which I have named, are at work with noticeable
energy and success among the operatives, but I

had no opportunity of observing their activities. The Unitarian pastor informs me that his church has some influence among the young mill people, " but it reaches very few, as you might naturally expect it would. It is not fitted to their appreciation, nor, perhaps, to their wants." He adds, " Being brought little into contact with the operative class, I can in general speak only from hearsay. in regard to them, and therefore should not presume to give an opinion to one who is searching for facts."

Many of the older operatives, especially among the English, Scotch, and Americans, are strongly influenced by what is called modern scientific thought, and have come to regard religion as something outgrown and antiquated for all intelligent persons, but still useful and necessary for the ignorant and inferior classes, — the common people. The strongest separative and unfraternal influence which I have encountered or observed in American life and thought is this tendency of " scientific thought " to produce a feeling of contempt for those who do not share it, — for " the unenlightened masses."

Several of the mill corporations of this city are embarrassed by indebtedness out of all proportion to their financial strength or available assets. Some of them have recently been forced to suspend payment, and it is probable that others will soon have a similar experience. These difficulties have been caused in part by embezzlements and defalcations, of which the city has had its share, within a few years, in common with most other places in our country ; but the popular judgment attributes far too large a proportion of the financial troubles of the mills to this source. Most of them have resulted from the effects upon business and industry produced by our civil war, and from the peculiar intellectual and psychological conditions which prevailed among our people for a few years after that convulsion. Usually these evils or embarrassments are the result of false or erroneous thinking. There was too much money invested in machinery for the manufacture of cotton goods, more than was required for all the business that could be done. More mills were built and equipped than could be employed with profit. These excessive and abnormal investments of capital in a particular branch of business were made because capitalists and manufacturers depended upon imaginary markets, upon a demand for cotton goods which was supposed to be practically unlimited.

The labor reformers insist that there can be no overproduction while any human want remains unsupplied. This is pure sentimentalism, worthy of the political economy of Rousseau, and has no scientific or practical quality whatever. What is more to be regretted is, that many of the writers of our time who are trying to aid the development of rational ideas on these subjects are themselves influenced, and much of their work is viti-

ated, by the same illusions which have made the
sentimentalists their prey. When we declare, in
poems, sermons, and optimistic essays, that men
everywhere should be able to possess and enjoy
whatever can add to the comfort, refinement, and
happiness of life, it has a delightfully generous
and philanthropic sound, and we are disposed to
feel that we have done something to hasten " the
good time coming." But the simple fact, of in-
expugnable strength, upon which the whole matter depends in actual business is that overproduction occurs whenever a manufacturer produces so
many more goods than he can sell that the amount
left upon his hands absorbs the profits of his business, or such a proportion of the profits as gradually to impair and lessen his productive capital.
Men do not manufacture cotton cloth, or grow
corn and wheat, or make newspapers, from motives of generosity or sentimental philanthropy.
They produce all these articles to sell them ; and
fraternal justice to the laborers employed, and the
use of whatever means can be applied for their
education, will give increasing productiveness,
security, and permanence to all these branches of
industry. But it will not do to make any kind of
goods merely because people ought to have them.
We might insist that life must be a condition of
squalid misery in every family where there is not
a seven-octave piano; but the manufacturer who
should therefore undertake to make pianos for all
who do not now possess them would soon be in a

13

position to give lessons to our political economists on the real nature of overproduction. It is not true philanthropy to employ men to make goods which cannot be sold. To do so must always result in the destruction of capital and the injury of the laborer. Of course, there are chances of loss by the production of unsalable goods which cannot be foreseen, but this only makes all possible foresight the more necessary. We have built many mills and bought much costly machinery for the manufacture of cotton and iron goods which nobody would buy. Some of these enterprises have already come to an end in necessary ruin. Others are deferring their fate by adding to an indebtedness which is already greater than the present value of the entire property or investment. Much of the capital thus invested is lost, and can never be recovered by any possible skill or ingenuity.

My friend the editor of the labor-reform newspaper holds that the best means for securing the rights of the laboring people, and obtaining a just remuneration for their labor, is the multiplication of their wants ; that is, they should be taught to live more and more expensively. He says that civilization consists in this constant increase in the number of the wants of human beings, and that we must encourage the working-people to demand and use so many things as necessaries of life for them that employers will be compelled to give them higher wages. But I think that all the facts which have any relation to the subject indicate that this particular element or tendency of civilization has already an excessive development, and that most persons in this country have already more wants than can possibly be satisfied. It would tend to greater clearness of thinking if people would remember that there is no evidence of any provision in the nature of things which assures us the possession of everything we may want. It does not appear that the earth contains materials for unlimited wealth, or that it will ever be possible for everybody to be rich and live in luxury. The earth does contain materials for subsistence for human beings, as long as there are not too many of them. But the overproduction of human beings is a frequently recurring fact in the history of the race. It is a possibility in nearly all civilized countries, and though it may not require attention here for a long time to come, it is certain that its recognition is already necessary in all systematic treatment of the chief subjects connected with political economy and national welfare.

I believe the labor reformers are in error in thinking that the continued and indefinite reduction of the hours of labor would be a benefit to the working-people; but I am aware that they have the support, in this view of the matter, of nearly all the political economists of every school. Most writers upon the subject eulogize the effect of labor-saving machinery upon the interests of the workingman, affirming that any inconvenience resulting from it is but temporary, and that the permanent effects are necessarily beneficial. It is constantly assumed, as if it were an indisputable certainty, that the less men have to work the better for.them. I cannot discover any necessity or provision in the nature of things which renders it thus certain that all devices and inventions which result in dispensing with human labor are to work advantage to mankind. It is time to challenge this assumption. It is entirely a question of fact, and *a priori* reasoning is here out of place. The most positive proof that labor-saving machinery is beneficial up to some certain point or degree of development and application cannot be safely accepted as evidence that its development and application can be profitably extended without limit.

I believe that for most men more than eight hours' work per day is required for the maintenance of physical, mental, and moral health. I think that for most men, including operatives, mechanics, farmers, and clergymen, more than eight hours' labor per day is necessary, in order to keep down and utilize the forces of the animal nature and passions. I believe that if improvements in machinery should discharge men from the necessity of laboring more than six hours a day, society would rot in measureless and fatal animalism. I have worked more than ten hours per day during most of my life, and believe it is best for us all to be compelled to work. It would be well, I think, if we could make it impossible for an idler to live on the face of the earth. Religious teachers are not without responsibility for having taught that the necessity of labor is a curse. The world owes most of its growth hitherto to men who tried to do as much work as they could. Its debt is small to the men who wished to do as little as possible.

The principal thing required in connection with these interests of our national life is, I think, that the operatives and other working-people shall have a better education, — an education which shall include some more adequate safeguards or defenses against illusion than are provided by the methods of culture and training now in common use in this country. As things are, it can scarcely be said that any effort is made to teach the working-people anything regarding their duties, rights, and interests as citizens, as Americans, except by the churches and the labor reformers. As religion is at present usually understood by its teachers in this country, it does not habitually give great prominence or emphasis to the cultivation of feelings of attachment, responsibility, and obligation to our country. It is commonly regarded as dealing with men only as individuals, and as accomplishing the elevation of society by improving the character of the units of which it is composed. Few, even of our best people, have now any vital feeling or sense of nationality, of our position and duties as Americans. Nor have I been able to find anywhere a clear exposition of the claims which our country has upon us all, of any service which the nation rightly demands of its children, except what is required in time of war.

I think the time will come (and should come soon) when the preparation and supply of suitable reading matter, as an instrument for the education and guidance of the working-people, will be regarded as a necessary part of the equipment of the manufacturers in a town like this. It is so now, but the prevailing optimism, being essentially unintelligent, and therefore wanting in flexibility, is not yet aware of the new conditions and tendencies in our industrial, social, and national life. The capitalists, manufacturers, and cultivated people of every town where there are one thousand operatives should unite in the publication of a small, low-priced newspaper for circulation among the working-people, — a paper conducted by some one who understands that the elements and tendencies of our national life cannot be adequately dealt with by the subjective method which most of our teachers now employ; by a man who sees clearly that the knowledge and recognition of the objective facts of human experience supply the only sufficient basis for wise action.

The use of such means for the education and guidance of the working-people would cost far less, in money even, than the present plan of letting things take their course. The confident expectation that an improvement or revival of business will soothe the discontent of the working classes, and relieve the country from anxiety regarding their action, which has become general within the last few months is, in part, the result of a hasty and superficial judgment of the facts of the time. There are many workingmen and teachers of workingmen in this country, believing in the absolute sovereignty of the laboring classes, who would not be rendered less active or determined in their campaign against the existing order of things by any possible degree of industrial prosperity. They believe in a different order of society, and hope to organize the wage laborers of the United States, and unite them in a persistent endeavor to modify the existing social and political order. They have more impulse and endurance than most of the supporters of our existing civilization, and also a better understanding of the necessity of adapting means to ends. They have also a measure of truth on their side, for the existing order and civilization cannot be defended as complete, or wholly just; they need improvement.

I wish to deal gently with the impenetrable inapprehension which thinks it a sufficient answer to all such pleas for an increase of activity on the part of cultivated people to say that the ignorant and visionary schemers who would like to overthrow our institutions can never succeed. Sarcasm here would be a waste of force. But intelligence can understand that some things short of absolute ruin are still so undesirable and in-

jurious that it is worth while to try to prevent
them.   The force by which the world has chiefly
grown hitherto is the love of excellence for its
own sake, the feeling of obligation to try to make
things better, to remedy injustice, and to remove
hurtful, enslaving ignorance whenever we can do
so.   But it is to be confessed that these are con-
siderations of little weight with the optimism of
our time.

It is not enough that people who have money
and culture pay the operatives their wages.   That
is not all that justice requires.   It is my belief
that, in the city of which I have here written,
the manufacturers were paying the laborers, at
the time of my visit, all that they could pay, and
that in some cases their wages absorbed the entire profits of the business.   But the working-
people are ignorant, and they are not taught as
they should be.   They are among the most valuable and indispensable of all the children of our
country.   Our national industry and prosperity
would be impossible without them.   Their life is
at best rather hard and uninviting, with little
room or means for the ameliorating, refining, and
sustaining influences which vary and brighten life
for many others.   There is far too little fraternal
interest in them, — too little disposition to share
their burdens, and to help them to make the
best of their life and of themselves that its inevitable conditions will allow.   We do not know
as much about them as we should.   Most people

think and care very little about the operatives, except when they threaten to make trouble. It is not safe or wise to allow so large a class to be so far alien and separate from the influences and spirit of our national life. I do not think the mill people are, as a class, inferior in morality, in the ordinary sense of that word, to any equally numerous class in this country. On the contrary, I believe they are superior in this respect to any class of men and women who do not work.

We ought to know more about this sort of people, about their circumstances, their ways of living, their thought, and the tendencies and effects of such a life as theirs upon character and civilization. As things are, there is nobody to speak for them. We should know more about what they do with their wages ; how much they are able to save, and to what extent they have the disposition to save anything from their earnings. I was very desirous to learn something of this last feature of their life in the city herein described; but although I visited all the savings-banks, and met everywhere gentlemen desirous of assisting me, nobody, so far as I could learn, had any knowledge of the amount of deposits by operatives in the savings-banks of the city. The matter had once been "looked up" as an electioneering measure, but the statistics had not been preserved. The mill owners thought the amount was very large, while the labor reformers, as we have seen, believed it was "practically nothing."

I received the utmost courtesy and kindness from all whom I met, without exception. In these qualities the city is not surpassed by any place I have ever visited. I am indebted to many persons there for invaluable assistance, and am most grateful to some who will never see what I have written.

PREACHING.

IT is to be observed that preaching is something in which perfection is not attainable. The highest excellence in this work is but an approximation. The object of preaching, expressed in the largest way, is the formation, culture, and development of human character, and the guidance of conduct or life, in accordance with the laws, requirements, and obligations of our moral nature or being. With this in view as the end, preaching employs, as an instrument or means, the presentation of religious truth and thought, especially — in Christian teaching — the truths and doctrines of Christianity; the chief source whence these are to be drawn being the Scriptures of the New Testament, with illustrations and helps from the Hebrew sacred books, and from the religious history and experience of mankind.

The essential or fundamental principles and truths of Christianity are not presented or expressed in the New Testament in the form of exact, definite, direct propositions, so as to be apprehended with equal readiness, success, and perfection by minds of every character; but these principles belong to a class of ideas which in some measure depend for their apprehension upon moral and mental conditions, upon states of the will, the heart, or the moral character. In the phrase of the New Testament, they are spiritual truths or principles, and must be spiritually discerned or understood. These principles of Christianity are in this respect like most of the ideas which are conveyed in poetry and by the forms of other kinds of art; that is, for their adequate reception a certain preparation in the quality or attitude of the mind, and in the character of the person, is necessary.

Ideas and truths connected with almost all subjects of serious human interest may be appropriately employed in preaching. Innumerable facts of science in all its great departments may be rightly used in sermons, when such facts and truths are dominated and subordinated by a spiritual or religious purpose. Anything which can be made to serve a spiritual end may be of use, but all the elements and materials employed in preaching should be fused by a central, controlling, religious idea and motive. This spiritual or religious idea is of course complex. On one side it has, of necessity, an intellectual character; that is, in so far as it consists of thought, or is expressed in the form and by the terms of thought. But preaching, when rightly considered and performed, is not chiefly intellectual, but religious or spiritual; that is, it concerns itself primarily and principally with those faculties of man's being which find expression in reverence, trust, and obedience. Preaching deals with the will, and with action or conduct, and it addresses the intellectual faculties for the sake of these objects. But man's being or nature is a unit, and if the culture of the intellect is neglected, the religious character becomes ill balanced, morbid, and unwholesome. The evils and dangers resulting from excessive development of the emotional element in religion, though less portentous now than in other ages, still require examination, and render necessary whatever safeguards knowledge and foresight can supply.

Let us endeavor to see clearly some of the characteristics of the spiritual or religious idea. One of its essential qualities is that it always transcends the sphere of the transient, special, or particular, and passes into the region of the permanext and universal. All teaching which is truly spiritual or religious maintains a constant and direct relation with a moral order which is universal and eternal. This order is always recognized or the belief in its existence is necessarily implied. The end, object, or purpose of all preaching or religious teaching is the production, development, or cultivation of obedience to the requirements of this moral order, of trust in its sovereign adequacy, and of harmony and conformity with it. The personality or character of man as a moral being stands within this moral order, and is related to it. This order existed before he began to be, and he is in some sense produced by it, and is a part of it. It is a peculiarity of man's being and of his relations to this order that he learns progressively of its existence, nature, and requirements ; that he can never know or comprehend it perfectly, or attain to a complete or finished harmony or unity with it. His nature possesses or includes the capability of endless approximation or advance toward a perfection of vital harmony and oneness with this order, which is never to be completely attained, but which constitutes, in every stage of his progress, a most powerful incentive, inspiration, and ideal.

The preacher's faculties being finite, and their work necessarily imperfect, it constantly results that he does not adequately distinguish between what is special, transient, and subordinate, and what is universal, permanent, and supreme. His work is here so much a matter of relative or comparative emphasis, its quality depends so largely upon the character, insight, and genius of the man himself, that no adequate rules or directions for its right performance can be given. Some men have minds so mechanical and unspiritual that it is impossible for them ever to learn to preach usefully, and it may be conceded that some representatives of this class have in almost every age found their way into the pulpit.

One of the chief dangers or defects of preaching in our time, in this country at least, is its tendency to become predominantly intellectual, to deal with all its materials by intellectual methods. The facts, truths, principles, and ideas employed and illustrated in American preaching to-day belong, in great part, to the domain of the intellect, and are of a nature to stimulate chiefly the intellectual faculties, and to be apprehended by them. They are not marshaled by a spiritual purpose to spiritual ends, are not fused or assimilated by any power of adequate spiritual vitality. Preaching of this intellectual kind consists largely of argument and discussion, and it therefore necessarily produces and cultivates chiefly activity of the intellectual faculties; that is, a mental condition or attitude of a critical or questioning character, a spirit of doubt. The religious spirit is essentially the spirit of trust and of obedience. The special tendencies and developments of thought which characterize our own age have been, in too great measure, reproduced in the preaching of the time. We have had too much of "preaching for the times;" that is, the preaching has dealt too largely with things which are recent and transient, with the superficial and particular rather than with the vital, permanent, and universal.

The deepest and highest powers of the nature of man respond only to spiritual or universal influences and ideas. Nothing is potent or vital enough to summon his faculties to their highest and best activity except a perception or revelation of his relations to the universal order, and of the duties proceeding from and depending upon these

relations. It is wholesome and good for man —
it feeds the very sources of his life — to stand
awed before the majesty and beauty of the moral
order of the universe and the strength of its eternal laws. It is not possible that his nature should
be so expanded, stimulated, and purified, or raised
to such perfection of vitality and action, by any
other influence. To produce and develop this perception is one of the most important objects of
preaching; but it is not attained by the method
of treating religion chiefly as a matter of knowledge, as something to be explained and understood, a theory or system of thought, to be defended by argument and sustained by refuting
objections.

There is much preaching in this country which
is a potent and valuable means of intellectual culture, but which has little of the religious or spiritual quality which should characterize Christian
preaching. Many of the most intelligent, active,
and influential ministers have for several years devoted much attention to the peculiar literature of
modern science; and they have reported to their
hearers the speculations and theories of the men
who write about science for the magazines and re-
views, regarding subjects which are most closely
and vitally connected with the religious and theological beliefs belonging to Christianity, and with
the principles, laws, sanctions, and obligations of
Christian practice and character. The dissolving
or disintegrating tendencies of modern scientific

thought have thus been to a great extent combined with the preaching of the time, and so conveyed into the minds of the people who make up the churches of this country. Multitudes have in this way been made acquainted with the skeptical elements and tendencies of the thought of the age, and have been brought to feel the force of the objections which materialism has recently urged against the doctrines of Christianity. In many cases the scientific, skeptical, and critical ideas thus presented have had more force with the hearers than the answers or refutations brought forward by the preacher.

Many of these scientific objections to the doctrines of Christianity have received far more attention than is rightly their due on any ground of intrinsic weight, value, or respectability; and many of the ministers of the country have thus assisted in the propagation of skeptical notions to an extent which has noticeably influenced the thought of the people. Many persons have been affected by negative and disintegrating ideas with which they would have had little acquaintance but for the carefulness and iteration with which these opinions have been presented in the preaching of the time. It is possible to have too much discussion in preaching. Hearers are convinced and confirmed, strengthened and established, rather by the thoroughness and strength of the minister's own beliefs, by their perception of the confidence

14

and certainty which he feels, than by his presentation of arguments against skepticism.

It is always necessary to distinguish between what is superficial and of slight significance in the thought of the time, and what belongs to the class of forces and ideas which work deeply and widely in the mind of an age, gradually producing important changes in opinion, and so, at length, modifying the structure of society and the civilization of nations or races. I suppose we must say that this power of distinguishing between the superficial and insignificant manifestations of popular caprice and the real spirit, thought, and voice of the age is something which cannot be taught, communicated, or learned in its entirety ; but all real culture assists the development of this discriminating judgment or estimate of the comparative value of the different products and tendencies of human thought. It is also important to observe that the study of history and acquaintance with the world's best literature are specially adapted to assist the formation of the intellectual character which is the basis of such judgment and the pledge of its value.

Christianity properly changes front from time to time, to meet new forms of evil and error ; and its continued existence depends upon this neeessary flexibility. What changes of relative emphasis in Christian teaching and practice are required by the new conditions of human life and its environment in our age is an important question, — the most vital and momentous, indeed, which can now engage the thought of Americans in connection with religious subjects. This is at once the real issue and the common ground between the conservative and the modern parties in the Christian church. One party emphasizes the value of what has been tried and has done good service in the past ; the other emphasizes the need of new weapons, and the advantages of a partial change of front. Neither party has clearly defined its own ground or aims, nor have the leaders on either side thought it necessary to understand the position of those from whom they differ. Nobody seems prepared, as yet, for any thorough examination or discussion of the subject.

It is especially easy, in a time when thought upon religious subjects is becoming less vital and spiritual, for men to imagine that there is great value in the use of terms and phrases which have lost their primary significance and vitality, even for those who utter them. The truths, facts, experiences, and forms of thought and expression which furnish the most varied, adequate, and valuable illustrations of the relations between man and the universal order, or Supreme Will, which are anywhere accessible to the preacher, are to be found in the Hebrew and Christian Scriptures. But the forms of expression used in these books have no magical value. They cannot be successfully used as charms or spells. Their mechanical repetition or pronunciation by the human voice does not necessarily, or in itself, benefit those who hear. The use of phrases drawn from these high sources is helpful and tends to edification only if they are employed appropriately, and in connections or relations in which they have actual meaning, truth, and efficiency. Many preachers with whom I am acquainted, even among those of most pronounced rationalistic tendencies, often appear to think there is great value in the mere repetition of Old Testament phrases and figures of speech. But in our time even church members read the Bible so little that such expressions are often unintelligible, and tend to obscure the thought of the preacher instead of illustrating it.

The preacher always deals most successfully with the special sins, dangers, temptations, and evils of any time by using, as the chief substance and texture of his teaching, the great fundamental, permanent, and universal principles and truths of the moral nature and life of man, as they are illustrated in human experience and in the moral aspects of the history of mankind. He may safely trust to the universal nature which is in man and over him to make nearly all necessary special applications of general moral principles and universal truths. It is rarely best to give very elaborate treatment to such themes as form the staple of the newspaper writing of the time, or the prevalent gossip of the community. Yet the necessary distinction here does not consist so much in the difference of the subjects presented as in the spirit and manner of their treatment. Many things can be profitably used as incidental illustrations which could not properly be employed as the chief topics or substance of a sermon. A minister of my acquaintance was once preaching on the subject of truthfulness, and after various illustrations of its importance in practice, and of the temptations to unveracity in modern life, he said, "It is not open to a member of this church to evade the payment of the tax on dogs by any falsehood or equivocation whatever." He passed at once to other topics, but this sentence produced important changes in the practice of the citizens of that community, and in the amount of the revennes of the town. It is not likely that the effect would have been so salutary if my friend had delivered a lecture on dogs, with interesting facts and illustrations from history and literature, though such a lecture would not have been greatly unlike some modern sermons.

One of the special dangers and defects of preaching in this country is connected with the popular liking for oratory in the pulpit, the demand for what is called eloquent preaching. The common American idea of pulpit eloquence is low and sensational. It means chiefly a rapid and emphatic utterance of sonorous sentences, with something extreme, paradoxical, and violent in the thought presented, though not much thought is required. People demand of the preacher that he shall arouse and excite them, and they enjoy with a kind of voluptuousness the temporary stimulus and thrill of emotion which the preaching causes. It results from the laws of mental action that preaching of this kind does not inspire conscientiousness, nor tend to practical moral activity. It necessarily produces and fosters mental conditions which are extremely unfavorable to spirituality of character and life.

This appetite for eloquence, working with other tendencies of the age, has helped to make the preaching in this country dramatic and entertaining, but, in large measure, unspiritual. This, I think, can be rightly regarded only as a calamity, a tendency opposed to the interests of religion, adapted to weaken and subvert it, and to lead the people who are influenced by it into a region where religion will be impossible or regarded as unnecessary. This is one of the most important among the unfavorable tendencies of the age. It has made preaching " more interesting and attractive to the masses," but this has been accomplished by sacrificing much that is essential in religion itself.

There is a peculiar peril in oratory or eloquence for the orator himself, and few of the idols of popular taste have escaped it. This is the temptation to say things which will arouse and excite people, and so give them the emotional thrill which they require the orator to produce, rather than the things that are true, and that would tend to acquaintance, on the part of the hearers, with

their own needs and duties, and to a more rigid
subjection of their practice to the laws of Christian morality. The preacher's own taste for truth
is dulled, and his power of perceiving and distinguishing it is gradually lost. Seriousness declines,
and the most solemn and sacred doctrines and
facts of Christianity come to be regarded merely
as materials for oratorical display. An enormous
egotism disorders all the preacher's perceptions of
fitness and relation, subverts reverence, and eman-
cipates him from moral obligation. His hearers,
on their part, make the emotional enjoyment
which they experience in hearing eloquent preaching a substitute for Christian conduct and character. Exceptional instances of this kind are chiefly
interesting and significant as indications of general tendencies.

The requirements of the people regarding the
social life and occupations of the minister form a
serious hindrance to the spirituality and useful-
ness of his work. His work demands, more than
almost any other, except, perhaps, that of poets
and artists, periods of solitude, of silent thought
and waiting, of receptive communion with the
universal and eternal within him and around him.
It needs, in a peculiar degree, a free, unfettered
condition of his faculties. This is indispensable
for the best performance of his work, for the production of the higher qualities in his preaching.
Many men have been able to enjoy this disengage-
ment of their faculties, this freedom for devotion

and allegiance to the Highest, in the midst of affairs, conditions, and circumstances which, to most observers, appear to have been highly unfavorable to such concentration of faculty. But only the man himself can ascertain and decide what are the necessary conditions for the most successful performance of his work. Yet there are very few persons in the churches of this country who appear to have any understanding or appreciation of this law of the minister's work. The people with whom the preacher lives in closest relations usually think they know much better than he how he should arrange and employ his time during the week ; and the popular judgment decides that most of his time should be devoted to drinking tea with his parishioners, to what is called "going about among the people, and making himself at home with them."

The history of Christianity shows that the ministry has never possessed great power or authority, or the church a high degree of spiritual vitality, at any time when ministers were accustomed to pass a great portion of their time among their people in ordinary social intercourse with them. It is one of the features of the life of our time that pastoral visiting, that is, short calls devoted to conversation upon religious subjects, has given place to ordinary social visiting and intercourse between the minister and his people. This change is closely connected with important features and tendencies of the religion of the age. It has had a great effect upon preaching in this country. The modern practice has made impossible, in great measure, the habit of solitary study, and has thus shorn the preaching of the time of the peculiar authority and impressiveness which belong to utterances which come from lonely heights of thought and experience.

As things are at present, the minister's hearers are to a considerable extent already familiar with his thought before they meet him at the church. He has been with them during most of the week, and has thus had little time for thoughts arising from beyond the circle of pleasant, worldly conversation. I concede willingly all that may be claimed for the influence of the clergyman in thus promoting culture and refinement among his people, and so aiding the development of a higher civilization ; but I wish to point out the fact that the minister has in this way lost much of power and authority for his work as a preacher, and it is this work which we are now considering. It is not visiting among the poor or sick that injures a man's power as a preacher, but the modern expectation that he shall spend most of his time among the agreeable people of his parish, who live comfortably and like to be entertained.

The preaching of the time in this country is as good as the people are willing to hear. Neither in the church nor out of it is there any considerable demand for better preaching. Where there is most intelligence or culture the chief desire in regard to preaching is that it shall be entertaining, and thus suited to attract many hearers who will help to pay the expenses of the church. Under the " voluntary system," as it is called, which prevails here, it would be very difficult to give the people any kind of preaching which they do not want. The persons who need to be taught, guided, and instructed thus fix the standard and determine almost wholly the character of the teaching which they are to receive. This is an incidental effect of the dominion of the masses, of our universal-suffrage arrangement of society. In very few of the churches or congregations in this country can there be any continuous or habitual religious teaching which the people do not approve. The standard, or ideal, as to preaching is usually higher among ministers than among their hearers, and many clergymen maintain a constant struggle against the injurious tendencies of the popular taste, and try to create in the minds of their hearers an appetite for the higher and more spiritual qualities in religious teaching. But the preaching of the country, like nearly everything else in our national life, is likely to become more and more completely representative of the culture, taste, morality, and entire character of the people who compose the churches. If this is the tendency, the character of the preaching will not thereby be elevated or improved.

At last, everything among us must depend upon the average or aggregate culture, character, and will of the people. They are the real source of everything in our national life, of whatever good we can hope to keep or establish here, and of all the evils which injure or threaten us. Their sovereignty has been commonly regarded as having its sphere and operation in political affairs. The ballot is esteemed its proper symbol and expression. It is time for us to recognize the fact that under this sovereignty of the people everything in the life and character of our nation, its institutions, religion, morality, culture, and civilization, are dependent upon the character, development, and will of the people. Our people are not yet prepared or disposed to permit or sustain such preaching as is needed for the purification and guidance of our national life, and the growth of a higher civilization.

The church is still a valuable conservative and vital agency in our national life, but it exhibits only such spirituality, moral illumination, and earnestness as are possessed by the people who compose it; and it is marked by all that is defective in their culture and character. Under the voluntary system, preaching in this country is, in fact and of necessity, almost exactly what the people who have money wish it to be. Most of the preaching needs improvement. Some influences which our national interests most imperatively require should naturally come from this source. They are not now supplied by any agency whatever. But the preaching of the country can

be improved, so as to make it more valuable to
the nation, only by elevating the popular taste
through an advance in the culture of the more intelligent classes of our people. No adequate in-
strumentalities for effecting such an advance are
yet in existence. The preachers of the country
could do much to prepare the way for a better
state of things if they would give earnest attention to the facts, conditions, and tendencies of our
national life, but the popular optimism is averse
to such study of the facts of the time. The teaching of the Bible in regard to preaching, especially
its marked emphasis of the idea that it is the
business of the preacher to proclaim the will of
God, to deliver a message from Him, to teach
the truth, whether men wish to hear it or not;
that he is to utter whatever his ultimate convictions of duty require him to speak, accepting
whatever of suffering or loss may be the result, —
this has great influence upon all manly and sincere young men in the ministry. It inspires them
with something of heroic feeling, and still, even
in our time, gives to this profession an element
of solemnity, an ideal quality, and a culture in
elevated sentiments not found in equal degree in
other professions or occupations, except perhaps
among artists. But it soon comes to seem impossible, under the conditions of our modern life, to
obey these principles, or to maintain an attitude
in any wise heroic, except in personal self-denial
on the part of the minister for the sake of his

work, and in the endurance of life-long pain and regret on account of the difficulty of keeping the Bible estimate of his work in sight even as an ideal. It would soon increase the vitality of religion among us in a marked degree, and greatly improve our national life, if the more influential clergymen would unite and coöperate in developing and disseminating scriptural ideas of the moral authority of the pulpit, and its rightful freedom from popular control.

The dangers to religion in our time, as well as to the moral interests of our country, are very grave ; but it is for the present nearly impossible to interest Americans in anything which depends upon the operation of general and complex influences, or far-reaching tendencies. Optimism discourages effort for improvement. It is a great maker of phrases, and delights in announcing that " truth and right must triumph in the end." It refuses to regard anything that may occur in the mean time as worthy of serious attention. Many are anxious, but comfort themselves with the hope that "things will remain about as they are " in our time, and that those who come after us may be wise enough to deal with the increasing difficulties of the next age. Nothing seems very important to our people unless it is of the nature of a catastrophe ; nothing arouses them to serious interest but the belief in the near approach of a terrible crisis. There is little love of excellence for its own sake among us at present, and we are generally not only indisposed to earnest, steady devotion to high ideals, but we are almost destitute of respect, veneration, and enthusiasm for those who have, in other times, lived in high and noble ways. One chief reason why the heart of the age is not more potently moved by the central personage of the New Testament story is the fact that men have, to a great extent, lost the power to recognize greatness and heroism in human character, as they have lost the faculty of reverence for moral grandeur.

We have reached a state of things, a stage in the evolution of thought, when a partial change of front on the part of Christianity is necessary to meet the forms of error and evil which have been developed under the new conditions of society in modern times. The enthronement of the masses, and the extension of man's acquaintance with the physical universe, — democracy and science, — these have been the principal agents in the production of a new environment for religion in modern life. Some considerable changes in relative emphasis in Christian teaching are imperatively required by the conditions that have been developed in society since the revival of learning. That such changes will some time be made appears to me, for various reasons, probable. But such changes are never wrought by Almighty power operating directly and without human agency. Neither are they produced by "the resistless influence of the laws of progress." They have hitherto been brought about very slowly, as the result of many small movements and efforts on the part of religious teachers, and of other persons interested in religion and in human welfare.

Other-world sanctions have to a great extent lost their force in Christian teaching, and in the thought both of Christians and of the people outside of the church. The influence of what are called the miraculous or supernatural facts of Christian history has also less potency in human thought than ever before. Neither the distant past nor the distant future awes, inspires, or restrains men now as heretofore. The church will be obliged to recognize these changes. The chief line or method of advance is by an increased emphasis upon the sanctions, obligations, and activities belonging to this world and to the moral life of the present time. Heaven can wait. It is not necessary to think much about it while we have strength and time for labor here. But this world ought to be purified, and life here developed, organized, and directed in obedience to the requirements of order and justice. And for us — for Americans — this world means our own country. We have no real opportunity or relation with humanity in general. As they are usually set forth in the phrases of sentimentalists, the brotherhood of mankind and our duty to humanity are abstractions without vital meaning or practical value. We have most vital relations, we have boundless opportunity, with the people of our own country. We need the influence of the strongest emphasis that religion can give to our duties as citizens, as members of the national family. Religion should translate the idea of the brotherhood of man into the idea and fact of the fraternity of the people of our country. Righteousness, justice, order, patriotism, — these are the principles which religion should henceforth emphasize in this country. If Christianity should come to mean this and do this, it would regain its lost vitality and sovereignty; it would be again a light to guide and a law to govern mankind.

But all the experience of the past makes it probable that such a change of front and shifting of relative emphasis on the part of Christianity will not be accomplished without enormous loss, injury, and moral disintegration. I do not know how much of this might be prevented if a few of our teachers and leaders were wise enough to begin at once to act upon the lessons which time is sure to teach; but there are few signs of such wisdom among us. The old beliefs are losing their power, but no new sanctions of equal or adequate vitality are taking the place of the convictions which are thus perishing. No human power can prevent this decay of the old beliefs, and no wise man could wish to hasten it. We need now insight and impulse for the development of the new methods and forms of thought and teaching, and the new ideas of life, which are to house and clothe, feed and guide, the "emancipated " but untaught multitudes, who, if left to themselves, are the helpless, predestined prey of the delusions always ready to ravage and desolate the life of a race or generation which has not inherited a vital and adequate religion.

Probably the most groundless and irrational of the teaching of our time is that of the "liberal" or "rationalistic" optimists, who insist that there is no loss of moral vitality, or decay of religion itself, in this wide-spread breaking down of the old beliefs. The history of times of transition in the past and the known laws of mental action and social change should lead us to expect a long period of intellectual bewilderment, of religious and moral disintegration and political debasement. We shall probably try many wasteful and hazardous experiments; the optimists will still prophesy triumphantly; and the people who live after us may learn, if we do not, that new agencies for the education of the people are indispensable, and a new consecration to the interests and objects of our national life. A few men will think of the flag with something of the passionate devotion with which men formerly thought of the cross, and will transmit their high ideal to their children as a holy trust, to be guarded and enshrined by each succeeding generation. After measureless toil and suffering, it may be found that Christianity has made a partial change of front, that men in this land have again a religion, and that civilization has moved forward to higher grounds.

15

I HAVE recently had much conversation, on subjects connected with politics and our national life and interests, with several thoughtful and earnest men in two of the principal New England States. Some of them are laborers in cotton mills; some are manufacturers and capitalists; others are farmers. Some are possessors of considerable property, and live in easy comfort, if not in affluence; others are very poor. There is a noticeable agreement of ideas or convictions among them in regard to some problems which are becoming more and more important for the people of our country. I asked the same questions of these representatives of various classes of my fellow-citizens; and the absolute identity, not only of thought or belief, but of the forms of expression, in most of the answers, indicates, I think, a pretty thorough indoctrination by the same teachers of the whole school or party holding these sentiments. I give, for the most part, my own questions, with the replies, which were nearly the same from all. Much of the language is reported exactly, from notes made while we talked. Some slight verbal changes were necessary, but the meaning is given as accurately as possible throughout.

The first question was, usually, " Do you think the condition of our country prosperous and encouraging ? " And the answer was, uniformly, " Not for the many, the mass of the people. There can be no real prosperity for our country under such conditions as now exist for laboring people."

" What do you regard as the chief dangers of our country ? "

" There are two great dangers. The first is the aggregation of wealth in a few hands, especially the aggregation of wealth in the possession of large corporations, in which ambitious and unscrupulous men use the power which money gives as a means' for the control of legislation and of public thought and its expression. The great moneyed corporations, or a few rich men in them, own all the influential newspapers, and they allow no thought opposed to their opinions or interests to reach the people. No one can speak for the interests of the people except through a few feeble and obscure journals. The control of the great moneyed corporations over legislation is, in our country, almost absolute."

" The other great danger is the growing belief in the necessity of a strong government, and the fear, even in the minds of good men, that the people cannot safely be trusted, and that some men must be kept away from the polls. There seems to be a growing tendency in the minds of literary men to regard universal suffrage as a failure, and

to wish the possession of the ballot to be confined
to a more select body than the whole people.   It
is believed that the history of republics shows
that every experiment in republican government
has ended in an aristocracy, — in the elevation of
a few men to complete control ; and that our system must have the same result and end. We have
already made some changes in this direction.
The cry is that the people of cities are not fit to
govern them.   There is a strong tendency in recent legislation to limit the right of suffrage in
the name of political purity."

" The two greatest dangers are the corruptions
of aggregated wealth, and the indisposition to
trust the whole people with a share in the government."

" All history shows that the many have never
done wrong to the few, but the few have often
done wrong to the many. All legislation by the'
people has been honest and fair to the few. History acquaints us with no instance to the contrary."

" Delusions never seize upon, possess, or mis-
lead the many, the mass of the people, but always
have their development and mischievous influence
in some select class, — among persons who are,
by their tastes or culture, separated from the mass
of the people."

" When a particular, select body or class of men
acquire what is now commonly called education
(it is usually partial and unpractical), they are

thereby enabled to impose their theories upon the people, thus deluding and enslaving the masses for the aggrandizement of their self-appointed guides. Massachusetts is, in greater degree than any other part of our country, the prey of delusions of all kinds, as she has more of what is called culture than any other State."

" But is not education or culture necessary to fit the people for the duties of citizenship, especially in our country, where problems so grave and difficult require solution ? "

" There is already sufficient intelligence in the possession of the mass of the people to enable them to govern wisely, justly, and beneficently, if they were not thwarted, misled, and oppressed by the few. The people go wrong, not from lack of intelligence, but from being deceived; and in this respect things are growing worse in our country. The people do not think, but allow editors to think for them."

" What can we do to hinder or prevent the aggregation of wealth in the hands of a few men, and in the possession of great corporations ? "

" When the fathers formed the constitution of our country, they did not imagine it possible that such evils or abuses could ever arise under its operation. We ought to have laws requiring the absolutely equal division of estates, at the death of parents, among all their children. We should adopt measures looking to the abolition of the corporate possession and management of wealth."

" All moneyed corporations should be dissolved, and, in time, their charters should be revoked. The constitution of the United States should contain an absolute prohibition of national corporations."

" We should repeal all laws that limit the right of suffrage; should make the ballot absolutely secret; and should give the ballot to every man simply because he is a man. No State should have power to limit the suffrage, or to exclude any class of men from the exercise of this sacred right."

" The many always know more than the few about every subject connected with the science of government and its practical working. Any ten thousand men know more than any one man."

" As to matters of national finance, we would have the government issue all the currency the people need in the form of paper money. Neither gold nor silver should hereafter be used as money. Our financial and industrial depression is the result of our having reduced everything to a gold standard of value. We have brought everything to a low value, that is, we have destroyed a great part of the wealth of the country, by making gold the standard, because there is not gold enough to go around. We have issued only enough greenbacks and paper money to produce some slight alleviation of our difficulties."

" The gold standard has paralyzed our industries. Money is invested by hundreds of millions in bonds at a low rate of interest. Nobody can engage in any productive industrial enterprise. There is frightful speculation in stocks and bonds of worthless companies, but nothing is undertaken that, if it were successful, would add to the real wealth of the country. Money is put into four per cent. bonds, because the gold standard has made it impossible to obtain any considerable profit from any legitimate business or industry."

" What we should do is to have money issued by the government according to the wants of the people. The government pays out some hundreds of millions of dollars each year to the people who work for it, — to soldiers and sailors, to clerks and officers, in its service. Let it pay them in its own paper money, which shall be used for all purposes for which money is needed, and shall be the only money of the country. Our opponents assert that we wish the government to give money to the people without equivalent or service from them, but this is not true."

" Money should be made of some material which has no intrinsic value, so that it cannot be made an article of commerce. Its sole value should consist in the government stamp upon it."

" The government should derive all its revenues from direct taxation, chiefly from the taxation of incomes, with taxes on tobacco, whisky, and other articles of luxury."

" Would you permit unlimited immigration from all parts of the world to our country."

"Yes; let everybody come who comes freely and of his own motion. All our troubles connected with immigration have resulted from imported labor, as in the case of the negroes and the Chinese. But those who are influenced by their own judgment to seek better opportunities for themselves and their children will benefit our country, not injure it."

"Is there no danger of our country's being over-crowded?"

"No; we have room and ample means of support for five hundred millions of people in this country. Our having assimilated so many races here, mingling the blood of all the principal nations of the world, is one of the chief causes of our superiority over all other countries and their people."

"Then you think Americans are superior to all other nations?"

"Undoubtedly. We are developing a higher type of manhood than has ever existed anywhere. Americans are more conscientious than any other people. The average intellectual character of our people is much higher and better than it was a hundred years ago. Our national morality is improving."

"How would you have the railroads of the country managed?"

"We should break up the corporations, and the railroads should be owned by the government. They should be made common highways, and every man who might wish to put a car on the road, and engage in the business of transporting freight or passengers, should be permitted to do so, under suitable regulations. The roads should be supported by taxation, if necessary. · It is absurd to say that a navigable river is a public highway, and belongs to the people, while a railroad which runs by the side of the river, along its whole length, cannot be a common highway, but must be the exclusive possession of a few men in a chartered corporation."

" What would you have the people taught in regard to morality, or the ground and standard of moral obligation ? "

" Temperance, industry, and probity constitute all the morality a man in this country needs."

" Is falsehood ever profitable to a man in public life, or to a political party ? "

" No man ever succeeds by falsehood. The man who uses it comes to an end. There is no political success, no future, for a man or a political party guilty of falsehood. Frank truthfulness is wisdom and strength. Pretense and concealment are folly and weakness. There never was a cause strong enough, or good enough, to sustain the injury of lying and dishonesty on the part of its supporters or advocates."

" What are your wishes in regard to our system of public education ? "

" We would not make much change. We would require every child to go to school, but would not teach a little of everything, as is done now. We would make education more practical, and more thorough in the branches of knowledge which would benefit the common people."

" Are your people generally optimists? Are you hopeful about our country's near future?"

" We are growing worse as to the impoverishment of the people. We have a greater number of men now who are enormously rich than ever before. These great aggregations of wealth make extreme poverty inevitable for the mass of the people. We do not expect speedy improvement. Perhaps there will have to be a great uprising of the people to right these wrongs. The ballot is the remedy for every evil and wrong in this country, and if the people can have the ballot they will make everything right. But if the ballot is withheld from any class, the people may take things into their own hands. We may be sure that the people will have their rights in one way or another."

" What kind of income tax would you approve?"

" We should tax all incomes, large and small, at the same rate. But we should define income as that which ' comes in ' from invested wealth. The earnings of labor and the profits on the business of a merchant should not be regarded as income. Dividends received for money which is no longer in the owners' hands, which are paid year after year to men who do nothing to earn them, should be taxed. They constitute real income. We should also have a heavy legacy tax. These arrangements would enable us to tax the income from bonds of every kind and class."

"Great accumulations of property in a few hands caused the downfall of Rome, and are now the worst curse of England. How soon the people may see these things, and assert their rights, nobody can tell, but all these reforms must come in time. There will probably be a great deal of trouble before the people open their eyes and take possession of their rights. At present the country is not proceeding or acting upon any rational system or method; we are merely stumbling, and tumbling, and wallowing along."

"What can be done to give the people greater advantages in connection with journalism?"

"We hope for electrical printing; for such advancements in science and invention, and such improvements in machinery, as will make printing so cheap that everybody can enjoy the advantages and opportunities which are now the exclusive possession of the very rich. There is no limit to what science may do for us. The earth is made for man, and all the powers and elements of nature are for his use and benefit. There is abundant provision for all human wants, if nature's rich gifts are not monopolized by the few to the exclusion and injury of the many."

"Are there some good and honest men who oppose you and your doctrines?"

" On, yes. The cultivated men do not believe in the people. We do. We trust the people. We think this country belongs to the people, and that they have a right to govern it. The Harvard men think we would ruin the country, but we only want the people to have what belongs to them."

" But would not your doctrines open the way to frequent and radical changes of our system of government, and thus imperil some things which are of great importance, — some things which are essential to our free institutions and our national life ? "

" The very essence and object of our system of government, as the fathers established it, is that the people shall govern, and shall make any changes which in practice or experience they may see to be necessary."

Having thus reported the opinions of my fellow-citizens as fully as possible in the form in which they were expressed in conversation, I wish to add some account of the impressions made upon me by the persons themselves. About the time of the close of our great civil war, or a little before, I had many opportunities of becoming acquainted with ideas and sentiments closely resembling those which are here described ; and since that time it has seemed worth while to study these tendencies and products of the intellectual life of our country directly, to converse with men of all classes and conditions of life who hold these opinions, in order really to know what they believe and seek, and upon what grounds they hold such convictions and cherish such aims. I have not adopted the judgment of their enemies, or that of their friends, in regard to the doctrines or the character of these men, but have sought to obtain first their own account of their principles.

I think these men are, as a class, thoroughly sincere in their opinions and sentiments regarding political subjects. They honestly believe what they profess, upon grounds which to them appear reasonable and sufficient. They manifest greater earnestness, or intensity of conviction, than is exhibited at present by the members of the other political parties of the country. This may result naturally from the fact that their party has never been in power, and that they are in consequence free from responsibility for the mistakes and evils of the time. They are likely to gain more and lose less than others by a frank avowal of their aims, even by the bold profession of doctrines which are generally regarded as extreme and dangerous. It is commonly remarked that both the old political parties are now somewhat wanting in earnestness, or strength of conviction, in regard to some important political doctrines. This is natural, and in a way inevitable, because both parties are manœuvring for position for the opening of the canvass preceding the next national elections. Probably the party managers do not greatly care upon what ground the contest is waged, if they can, at the beginning of the fray, secure advantages which will give them hope of "breaking the enemy's line, and throwing his forces into confusion." They do not, on either side, quite believe the dreadful things they have been saying of their adversaries. What I wish here to point out is that, while this manœuvring and the want of moral earnestness which it reveals are, under the circumstances, inevitable, and required by the necessities of political warfare, such tactics have certain disadvantages and embarrassments connected with them, from which our friends of the third party are entirely free. Boldness and frankness are elements of power in their appeal to the people. These men have more of sentiment than any other political class, and can more readily and successfully appeal to " the great American ideas of freedom and the rights of man." They are the natural heirs of some of the heroic elements and influences which formerly belonged to the attitude of the anti-slavery people. Upon examination this will be found a matter of considerable practical importance. I think that our fellow-citizens of this class may be said to be characterized by amiable and generous qualities. They are usually possessed of benevolent dispositions and strong sympathies. They all hold extremely hopeful and optimistic views of human nature, and sincerely believe that the common people are sages, saints, and heroes.

As to their thought or doctrines, these friends

of ours have remarkably clear and definite ideas
in regard to the objects of their efforts, and the
means by which they expect to attain them. They
believe that nature has provided abundantly for
the wants of all her children, that the earth
rightly belongs to the people, and that if men
were not wrongfully deprived of their heritage all
would live in comfort. Happiness is the object
of human life. Man has a natural right to happiness, but the masses are robbed of their rights
by the misrule and oppression of the few. They
believe that excessive toil is one of the chief
causes of unhappiness among the people, and they
intend to shorten the hours of toil. They think
that the labor of the common people is inad-
equately paid, and that the capitalist receives far
too large a proportion of the profits of labor, and
they intend to transfer a considerable proportion
of these profits to the laborer himself. They believe that unhappiness and pain, weariness and
poverty, can be in a very great measure abolished,
and they mean to accomplish this by reorganiz-
ing society under the rule of the common people.
They think it entirely right to change all constitutional provisions or other features of our system
of government which are found to obstruct the
will of the people, and that such changes should
be made as often as the people may think it necessary, and in such ways as the people may prefer.

These friends of ours believe that the people,

as they are, are capable of governing rightly and wisely, and that if they had the power in their hands their rule would always be just and beneficent. They think the notion that there is anything very difficult in the science of government or its practical administration, which requires peculiar wisdom, or culture superior to that possessed by the mass of the people, is a fiction, an invention of the oppressors of the people, by which they seek to strengthen their wrongful rule over the masses. They hold that " the hearts of the people are always right; " that the people love justice with a passionate and enthusiastic worship, that they are superior to all such unworthy and injurious passions as revenge, greed, envy, and selfishness, and that they are as wise as they are good; that the best dreams and ideals of poets and prophets are realized in the character of the common people of our country.

In conversing with my countrymen who cherish these sentiments and opinions, I am constantly reminded of Rousseau. Their ideas, and even their phrases and forms of expression, are often identical with his. I quote a few sentences from the " Émile " (Nugent's translation, London, 1763):

" Conscience affords greater light than all the philosophers; we have no occasion to read Cicero's Offices in order to learn to be honest." (Vol. ii. p. 271.)

" It is evident to the last degree that the learned societies of Europe are no more than public schools of falsehood ; and there are certainly more errors propagated by the members of the Academy of Sciences than are to be found among a whole nation of savages." (Vol. i. p. 304.)

" It is in vain that we aspire at liberty under the protection of the laws. Laws! Where are they? And where are they respected? Wherever you have directed your steps, you have seen concealed under this sacred name nothing but self-interest and human passions. But the eternal laws of nature and of order are still in being. They supply the place of positive laws in the eye of the man of prudence ; they are written in the inmost recess of his heart by the hands of reason and conscience ; it is to these he ought to submit in order to be free." (Vol. ii. p. 392.)

" It is the common people that constitute the bulk of mankind ; the rest above that order are so few in number that they are not worth our consideration." (Vol. i. p. 339.)

" You should therefore respect your species : remember that it is essentially composed of the common people ; that if all the kings and philosophers were to be taken away, they would not be missed, and affairs would be conducted as well without them." (Vol. i. p. 341.)

" Were we to divide all human science into two parts, one common to the generality of mankind, the other particular to the learned, the latter would be very trifling compared to the former." (Vol. i. p. 48.)

16

It is not probable that these resemblances of thought and language proceed from familiarity on the part of my friends with the writings of Rousseau. Few of them, I suppose, have read anything from his pen. Such thoughts and ideas have arisen naturally in their minds, as they did in his. These opinions and beliefs regarding the political and social interests and relations of mankind have been produced or developed here anew by the conditions of our national life. If we consider the circumstances of our people, their education and experience, and the natural and necessary effect of democracy, or the universal suffrage arrangement of society, I think we must expect a general development of such doctrines among the masses, and that the influence of these tendencies may possibly become so wide-spread and potent as to subject our system of government and the structure of society in this country to a very considerable strain. We shall not understand the causes, direction, or power of these ideas while we regard their development and career among us as accidental or anomalous. Their appearance and growth result from causes adequate to produce them. The phenomena attending their operation are not likely to be so transitory as to make examination difficult. We shall probably have time to study them.

Our friends appear to think that men of wealth and culture are of a nature essentially different from that of " the people." They always speak of them as belonging to a different class, and as being inspired by motives, passions, and principles entirely unlike those of the people. They think that the circumstances and position of men of property and culture, and the effect of the system of social and political organization under which they have so much power, necessarily make them selfish, grasping, unjust, and oppressive. They are convinced that there is no reason to hope for the improvement of society while the men of wealth and culture retain control, and are therefore determined to displace them. I am obliged to say that, while our fellow-citizens thus contemn culture, many of them have about as much of what now goes by that name as is possessed by most of those who belong to the " cultivated classes." So in regard to their ideas of wealth : they think it dangerous under the existing system and order of things, — likely to produce extreme selfishness, and alienation from the cause and interests of the people ; yet some of them are themselves capitalists, and possess the means of enjoying what they denounce as luxury when it is exhibited by those who are not " of the people."

It is curious and interesting to note the frequent resemblances between the doctrines which I am now examining and the fundamental ideas and assumptions of much of the best literature which our country has produced. That part of our national literature which contains the direct

expression of opinions in regard to the nature of
man, the principles of social and political order,
the genius of our institutions, and the true meaning and mission of America is almost all intensely
optimistic, and it supplies great store of maxims
and arguments of the highest dignity and respectability, which would serve as most convenient
weapons in the hands of our friends against many
features of the existing order of things.

One of the most important and characteristic
elements of influence in the movement which I
am describing is to be found in the ideas regarding
science which are held by this class of our people,
and propagated by their teachers. They expect
a millennium of universal plenty and happiness,
a golden age, under the dominion of science. No
imaginable invention for producing food, dispensing with labor, or creating wealth appears to
them impossible. If a great inventor should an-
nounce that he had discovered a method by which
he could evolve from a pail of water power sufficient to drive a freight-train from New York to
San Francisco, or that by establishing connections
between the opposite corners of a square league
of desert and the poles of a powerful electrical
battery he could in a few hours change the barren
sands to soil of matchless fertility, many of these
friends of ours would say, truthfully, that they
had long expected such achievements. Their
faith in " positive and negative electricity " would
scarcely be staggered by any possible story of

miraculous power or performance. They know of no reason why anything which they would like to have done for them should not be accomplished by means of this wonderful natural force; or, indeed, why any human want should remain unsupplied. Their ideas and methods of thought in regard to science, and the expectations which they cherish respecting the deliverance of mankind from the necessity of toil by means of scientific invention and discovery, are becoming important factors in our political and social conditions.

I have observed that the men in comfortable circumstances, who hold these doctrines, usually appear to feel but little personal enmity or bitterness against the classes whom they denounce. They say it is the system which is to be condemned, rather than the persons who sustain or administer it. But many of the poorer men and laborers seem to feel a degree of exultation in the prospect of the overthrow of the classes who, as they declare, have so long oppressed the people. All classes of believers in these doctrines are convinced that if the people are much longer thwarted and oppressed; if the ballot, which would enable them to right all their wrongs by peaceful means, is kept out of their hands, or its effect neutralized by the machinations of the money power, then the masses will rise in their might, and crush at once the system which is the source of their adversity. Most of them appear to feel a kind of sadness in view of the terrible suffering that may necessarily precede the coronation of the people, but they think it is all fated and inevitable. This mood, now becoming so common, is one in which many things are possible.

I see nothing to prevent the rise of a leader of this class, — of a man who, despising culture, shall possess as much of it as most of his antagonists, and, while denouncing wealth as the chief source of danger to the liberties of the people, shall himself be rich; who, holding these political and social doctrines in sincerity, shall advocate them with enthusiasm. If such a man should appear, and should add to these means of influence the potency of attractive social qualities, great kindness of heart, readiness of resource, commanding eloquence, and a stainless personal character, it may be that under such circumstances these ideas would attract more serious attention than they have yet received from our teachers and leaders.

Some of the opinions and sentiments here described appear to me erroneous and untrustworthy. The fundamental doctrine of the divine right of the people, for instance, as taught by our friends, is but the old doctrine of the divine right of kings in a new form. Its essence is unchanged. Under the new conditions of national life which accompany democracy, or result from it, the doctrine means the divine right of the majority. And as the believers in the divinely appointed rule of kings hold that the king can do no wrong, we are witnessing the development, under democratic forms of government, of the doctrine that the people — that is, the majority — can do no wrong; that the people are always unselfish, patriotic, and incorruptible, and possessed of wisdom adequate for every emergency, rendering injustice and serious error impossible under their sway. Now this doctrine of the divine right of a ruling class, and its supernatural equipment with all needed virtues, is a crude and barbarous conception, belonging naturally to the prehistoric or savage conditions of society under which it had its rise and development. It does not appear to have been improved by presenting it in its modern form, in association with democracy, nor can I learn that any new reasons or arguments have been brought forward in its support.

If this doctrine is true, then in a state composed of one million citizens, divided into two parties by their political opinions, five hundred and ten thousand men might constitute the party of the people. They would of course be in the utmost degree wise and just, and the four hundred and ninety thousand opposed to them would be unwise, and misled by dangerous error, if they were not selfish and corrupt. If the people are wise and right, those opposed to them must be foolish and wrong. But as a matter of fact it frequently happens that the foolish minority is able to convince and win over a small portion of the majority; and then the minority, without any change of principles, character, or aims, itself becomes the divinely authorized majority. That is, those who were last year the enemies of the people are now, though cherishing the same purposes which so recently made them dangerous enemies to liberty, themselves the people, and the only true friends of freedom. At the same time, some hundreds of thousands of men, who were last year members of the wise and virtuous majority, though still battling as earnestly as ever in support of the ideas which were then the perfection of wisdom and virtue, now constitute a deluded minority, and are the only "enemies of the people." No, friends, majorities are often wrong. The people are sometimes in error in regard to very important practical matters. They are sometimes ill informed and influenced by prejudice and passion, and are consequently unjust. There was a time when the people believed that the sun went around the earth every day. It is most probable that for ages the whole human race believed human sacrifices to be right. If the people are right today, they must often have been wrong in the past, for they have changed their beliefs again and again under the influence of advancing culture. Though they may be wiser than ever before, there is nothing to support the assumption that they have become infallible. The theory that the dominion of the people will secure mankind against all dangerous error, and abolish the evils which now afflict society and imperil civilization, is a convenient fiction.

Is it true that " any ten thousand men always know more than any one man " ? If one man were instructed in navigation, would he not know more about it than ten thousand men who had never seen a boat, or water enough to float it? A similar question might be asked in regard to the art of printing, the science of chemistry, the profession of law, and many other things. Does not any one man who can speak, write, and teach the German language correctly know more about it than any million of men who have never heard or seen a word of it? The art of government, of organizing the life of a nation and administering its affairs, is not the simple and easy task which our friends assume it to be ; it must rather be one of the most complex and difficult of human achievements. To persuade the persons who are intrusted with the government of a country like ours that their work requires no serious preparation or sense of responsibility is to propagate a most dangerous delusion.

Our friends regard the production and perpetnation of wealth as being due almost entirely to labor. They often say that laboring men — as distinct from the class of capitalists and cultivated people — have created the wealth of the country, and it is sometimes added that it justly belongs to them. The working people do not generally understand how much the production and existence of wealth depend upon other elements than mere muscular exertion. They do not.appreciate

the part which is performed by cultivated men
and capitalists in organizing and equipping business enterprises, in adapting production to the
markets of the world, and in so directing the
labor of multitudes of men and the use of costly
machinery as not to impair the capital invested.
They do not even understand clearly that the destruction of capital ruins the laborers of the country by destroying the business which gives them
employment. Many laborers think they are in
some way benefited by all the losses sustained by
capitalists. Wealth is not so stable or permanent
as our friends believe. It is of a sensitive nature,
and does not bear rough handling. It is easy to
destroy the value of any kind of property or investment by injurious legislation or mischievous
municipal administration. But many men believe
that by means of legislation "in the interests of
labor," and by severe taxation, most of the wealth
now in the possession of rich men and corporations can be transferred, without impairment, to
the hands of the working people. I think the
actual result, if their plans could be carried out,
would be the gradual annihilation and expulsion
of the wealth of the country. There would no
longer be any disparity of conditions between rich
and poor, because all would be poor alike. Our
organized industries would be destroyed. All machinery which requires the coöperation of many
laborers would be disused, and we should be
obliged to return to the conditions and methods

of life of the days before the introduction of improved labor-saving machinery, when the people
of our country depended almost wholly upon agri-
culture and such manufactures as could be carried
on in their homes. The world's wealth will not
be perpetuated or reproduced if the essential conditions under which it has been created are destroyed.

Might does not make right or justice on the
side of the people, any more than on that of the
tyrannical few who are regarded as their oppressors. Excessive taxation is robbery, though the
guilt and dishonor of it may be distributed among
millions of voters. When the people make a law
which compels the capitalists of a city to deliver
up their wealth at the doors of the city treasury,
for distribution among the laborers of the mu-
nicipality, in the form of unnecessary and dishonest appropriations for improvements, the act is
not more honest because committed by the people
under the forms of law. It is not wise to teach
the people of our country that nothing in their
political action can be wrong or unjust; that robbery and injustice are to be accounted right when
perpetrated by the majority by means of the ballot.

The beliefs of our friends regarding Nature or
Providence, and the attainable objects and ideals
of human life, are natural in the earlier stages of
mental and social development. They are the
products of subjective conditions, of what people

call their own intuitions. Strong and passionate
desires, unchastened by reason or experience, are
regarded as evidence that whatever they crave has
been specially created for their gratification. It
is held that " men have a right to be happy, have
a right to the possession of whatever will satisfy
their nature." Here, again, our friends are in
error in regarding the order of human life, or the
system of universal being, as something extremely
simple and transparent. It is not so easily ex-
plicable. We are of such a nature that we want
many things, but I cannot find that there is any
provision or arrangement in the order or laws of
nature for our having whatever we want. Much
of the popular teaching about the wise and beneficent adaptation of everything to everything else
in the universe, the relation between all natural
wants and the means for satisfying them, and the
wonderful economies of Nature rendering waste
and failure impossible in her domain, is pure assumption, and will not bear examination. We do
not really know so much about these matters as
many people suppose. Whether we talk of the
bounty of Nature or the wisdom and goodness of
God, the difficulties are the same. The subject
is too deep for us. It is pleasant and comfortable
to believe that everything is made for our happiness, and that the universe is pervaded and
controlled by a wise and omnipotent tenderness.
But as a matter of experience and fact, there is
measureless pain in the world, failure and cruelty,

hideous and uncompensated wrong and suffering. Life is a stern, hard service, and the wisest and noblest have learned to think little about happiness, and to give their strength to the work of the day, because "the night cometh, when no man can work." I have myself tried living for happiness, and have found that the effort, even when successful, tends to disintegration and chaos. My observation of the lives of others convinces me that these doctrines which lead men to feel that they have a right to be happy, and that they are wronged and oppressed unless they have everything they want, are the result of defective analysis. The people who hold this philosophy of life are sincere, but their thinking is erroneous. It does not follow that we are to make no effort for the deliverance of mankind from injustice and oppression. To right what is wrong, and improve the conditions of human life, is the noblest work to which we can give our hearts in this world. But our friends of whom I am now writing fail in large measure, and injure their own work, because they have not given sufficient attention or patience to the endeavor to understand the difficulties that lie in our way. It is not so easy as they think to know what are the best means for bringing about the changes which all good men should desire to see accomplished. Our friends especially need more knowledge, in order to be able to discriminate truly between objects that are really desirable and attainable and those which human passion naturally craves in its early, " unchartered freedom," but which are either impossible of attainment, or of a nature to cause injury and loss when attained.

This brings me to the error of our friends in rejecting and denouncing culture. They might do good by exposing what is crude, superficial, and unpractical in what goes by the name of culture, and by expressing their sense of the need of something better. If the working people would thoughtfully try to understand what is defective in the education of their class, and would give their countrymen their judgment regarding what is most needed for the equipment of their own children for their place and work in life, it would be a valuable service. If the state undertakes the education of the children of the people, as it does in this country, I think the working men have a right to claim for their children the best education the state can give; that is, such an education as will in the largest measure possible fit them for the work and experience of their life. The people of our country, without exception or distinction of classes, need more knowledge and better education. The people of wealth and culture have much to learn and to do. They do not yet understand how insecure is their own position. They have little real knowledge of the new conditions of society in this country. The people of whom I have here written are not wholly wrong. They have some measure of truth and right on their side, some reason for discontent. Our politics are deficient in patriotism, and our partisan leaders have too little interest in the welfare and guidance of the people. The people of wealth and culture need a closer acquaintance and association with the working people and the poor. They generally lack something of the fraternal spirit which they should feel, but they are especially wanting in the manifestation or expression of such kindly and fraternal feelings as they really have in their hearts. The workingmen misapprehend the people of wealth and culture. There is, indeed, mutual misapprehension and want of acquaintance between the working people and their employers. If the opinions of the masses are wrong and their aims impracticable, it is worth while to do far more than has yet been done in this country to show them how they are wrong, and to teach them whatever fundamental principles are available for their guidance. There is too much impatience shown by many of our writers and leaders because the masses do not learn more rapidly, are so persistently wrong-headed, etc. What is the value, after all, of the culture which qualifies us to dispute learnedly regarding the chief social and political tendencies of the people of ancient Greece and Rome at every period of their history, but does not equip us for any real study of the life of our own time and country, nor enable us to understand the growth of destructive tendencies in the society

of which we are members? It is most mischievous to assume, as is constantly done on both sides,
that some of the different classes of our people are
already so completely separate and distinct that it
is next to impossible for them to understand or influence one another. It is the assumption of those
who are too indolent to study the facts of our condition. The cultivated people have not yet made
a tithe of the effort to teach the working classes
which is necessary to prove whether they can be
taught or not. There is great unteachableness,
not only among the working people, but in the cultivated classes; yet no large class in this country
is hopelessly inaccessible to teaching, or insuscep-
tible of guidance. (Could not something be done
in the way of increased publicity on the part of
their managers regarding the essential features,
methods, and conditions of the great business and
manufacturing enterprises of the country, so that
workmen could better understand the justice and
necessity of the course of action pursued by their
employers?)

It is somewhat strange and ominous that so
many cultivated people should insist, apparently
with a degree of pride, that they are themselves incapable of addressing the working people so as to
be understood by them; that they have no power
to establish such relations with them as would
enable them to influence their opinions. When,
a few months ago, I suggested — with other measures for producing a better understanding between

the different classes in our country — the publication, by those who believe in property and in culture, of a good, low-priced newspaper for circulation among workingmen, there were emphatic protests from prominent journalists, who assured me that a newspaper dealing with the life and wants of operatives, if edited by capitalists, manufacturers, and cultivated people, would certainly fail of influence among the class whom it would be designed to benefit, for the reason that their inevitable aversion to everything bearing the stamp of capital would strangle the well-meant enterprise at its birth. This indicates want of acquaintance, on the part of such writers, with the feelings, spirit, and character of our working people. There is not yet any such incurable alienation and hostility between the workingmen and their employers, the capitalists of the country. There is much misunderstanding, and some of the facts of our condition are gravely unfavorable; but they do not by any means sustain the despairing conclusion that no direct effort to enlighten and convince the workingmen would be of any avail. My own opinion is that the workingmen are, as a class, quite as accessible to teaching or enlightenment as our cultivated optimists.

In endeavoring to understand the spread of false and hurtful ideas among the workingmen, we observe, first, that these beliefs arise naturally and legitimately in many minds under such conditions as have prevailed here during the last

17

eighteen years. In the next place, we should recognize the fact that many persons have devoted themselves with remarkable zeal, energy, and success to the propagation and inculcation of these opinions and sentiments. The chief remaining feature in the matter is the entire absence of corresponding or adequate activity on the part of those who should feel most interest in preserving and extending whatever is valuable in the results of our civilization. In this inaction, this want of coöperation and of direct effort for the propagation of their own convictions, on the part of those who believe in property and culture, and in the value and necessity of constitutional government, is the chief source of danger for our country. All these interests are seriously imperiled, not alone by the ideas of the working class, but by the general operation of disintegrating influences in our society, and by the want of better training and principles, and higher character, among all classes of our population. The dainty and querulous tone of many who should be among the teachers and leaders of our time shows that the disorganizing influences of the age are already affecting the cultivated classes, and diminishing our national vitality.

There is great need of wise and effective resistance to the attack upon constitutional government. Most of our people need a better understanding of the necessity of some accepted principles and system of national organization and administration, which shall not be subject to change at every election. Some of the strongest tendencies of the time lead in the direction of the absolute empire of the majority, without restriction or limitation from any source whatever, — the rule of the caprice of the hour, and the entire repudiation of all precedents, pledges, charters, and constitutional regulations and provisions. We have adopted universal suffrage to begin with, and now we must prepare for it afterward. The essential and distinguishing feature of our system is that it is government by the people. But the mere adoption of this system of government does not confer upon the people the wisdom which they need for its administration. That must be obtained by other means. Our system was not devised by its founders to introduce and maintain the absolute and tyrannical rule of mere majorities, though this view of its purpose and character is now urged with great vehemence. It was meant that changes in our political methods should be made slowly, and that they should not extend so far as to destroy the organic character of the national government.

If the people who do not approve the doctrines I have here described are in earnest, it is necessary that they should learn to address the masses. Those who believe that property and culture are essential to our civilization must present their case. They and their interests are on trial, and it is time for them to plead the cause of what they

most value. It is not a matter of extreme difficulty. Surely our cultivated men should be able
to speak intelligibly to the whole nation and to
every class it contains. To admit that capitalists
and cultivated men cannot gain the attention and
confidence of the workingmen implies distrust of
the justice and reasonableness of the principles
and position of the conservative class. Americans
who feel that their cause is a righteous one should
not fear to speak for it before their own countrymen. I have had considerable experience in writing for the working people to read, and have
found that they can understand plain speaking
and sincerity. If I had the money required for
such an enterprise, I should at once proceed to
establish such a newspaper as I have recom-
mended. What we most need cannot be accomplished by ordinary political journalism, though
political parties are necessary and useful. The
need of the time is the education of the people
in the principles and duties of American citizenship and fraternity. I have not attempted a complete examination of these subjects,—that is a
work for the people of our country; but I have
hoped to bring about a more general and thorough
discussion of these questions of the time. I am
not devoted to any particular plans or measures
for improvement. I should be glad to see each of
my suggestions set aside for something better.

Lightning Source UK Ltd.
Milton Keynes UK
UKHW022118211118
332759UK00018B/1929/P